AF711606

Kafka Up and Running for Network DevOps

Set Your Network Data in Motion

Eric Chou

Kafka Up and Running for Network DevOps

Set Your Network Data in Motion

Eric Chou

ISBN 978-1-957046-03-7

© 2021 Network Automation Nerds, LLC.

Tweet This Book!

Please help Eric Chou by spreading the word about this book on Twitter!

The suggested tweet for this book is:

I just bought Kafka Up and Running for Network DevOps, let's keep data flowing!

The suggested hashtag for this book is #NetDevOps.

Find out what other people are saying about the book by clicking on this link to search for this hashtag on Twitter:

#NetDevOps

For my family, you are my 'why' for everything I do.

I would like to thank the open-source software community. My life would be very different without the many dedicated, talented individuals in the open-source community. Thank you all.

Contents

Introduction

Welcome to the world of data!

Unless you have been living under a rock for the last few years, you know data processing, machine learning, and artificial intelligence are taking over the world. Data exists everywhere around us. We can now check real-time traffic information from online cameras before we even leave the house. We can connect to our thermometers remotely to automatically adjust house temperatures. Better yet, the thermometers can also be self-taught so that they can adjust the temperatures all by themselves. Before our family weekend movie nights, my kids love to leverage the WiFi-enabled lights to match the lighting with our mood.

How do these cameras, lights, and thermometers able to take measurements and generate data? It turns out the cost of small sensors and tiny computing units have been coming down steadily since the early days and now can be integrated into everyday items. However, the generated data by one or two devices might not be sufficient enough to yield meaningful results. After all, traffic information on one street might only benefit a tiny fraction of people who travels on that street, but aggregated traffic information on all streets can help everyone. Generally, it is by aggregating all disperse data sets across hundreds of devices; we are able to derive useful information that helps us with our daily lives. The data are constantly flowing between producers and consumers of data.

Have you ever wondered how these data are being exchanged between data producers and consumers? Does each of the devices provide an API (Application Programming Interface) to be queried? Do each of them have local databases that persist the data? What about data integrity, transmission latency, or scalability?

There are many tools and projects that address these data streaming and exchange issues. One of the most popular open-source tools widely used by companies large and small alike is Apache Kafka[1].

What is Kafka

You might be thinking, "Don't we already have lots of data storage systems? Why do we need yet-another-storage-system?" You are right, and we do have lots of storage solutions such as relational and non-relational databases, cache systems, big data storage clusters, search solutions, and many more. But in most of the data storage cases, the data is entered in once, stored in the database, then retrieved later when needed. For example, when I visited my dentist for the first time, they asked for my personal information, entered them into a database so for my future visits, they could pull up my record. This is very different than the traffic sensor data example that we discussed.

What sets Kafka apart is it was built from the ground up to treat data as continuous flows of information that are constantly being produced, enhanced, manipulated, and consumed. Instead of a focus on holding in data like databases, key-value stores, search indexes, or caches, Kafka architects itself as a system that allows data to be a continually evolving stream of information.

According to the Apache Kafka project page:

> *Apache Kafka is an open-source distributed event streaming platform used by thousands of companies for high-performance*

[1] https://kafka.apache.org/

data pipelines, streaming analytics, data integration, and mission-critical applications.

Companies known for a large amount of data, such as AirBnb, Datadog, Etsy, and many others across different industries, use Kafka to build their data pipeline. These data pipelines use a variety of services that both produce and consume data in a continuous format.

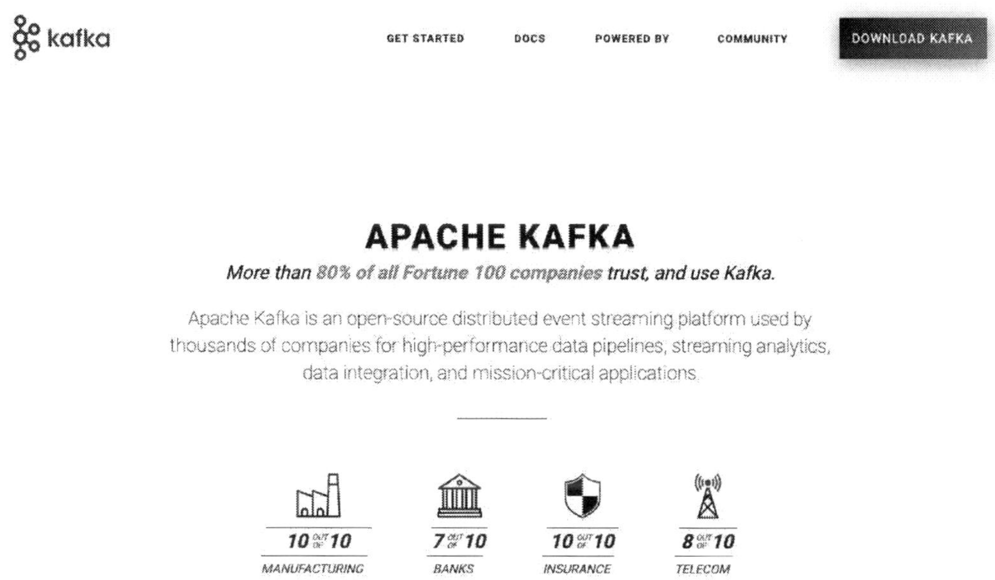

Figure Intro. 1: Powered by Apache Kafka (https://kafka.apache.org/powered-by)

Don't worry if you have not heard of Kafka before or are not sure how, as network DevOps engineers, this tool can help us. We will go a lot deeper into Kafka in this book.

Why do we need Kafka

As a general overview, there are many uses cases for Kafka in network engineers:

- We can use Kafka to stream data, such as logs and NetFlow data, once and be consumed by multiple receivers. Kafka takes care of the ordering of messages, acknowledging receipt to producers, delivery confirmation to consumers, and balancing the data between different recipients.
- We can separate data into logical partitions called *Topics* in a single Kafka cluster. This allows subscribers to only receive the data they are interested in, so the log receiver will not need to receive flow data.
- Kafka allows for an event-driven architecture, such as triggering events based on different types of events. For example, a log receiver can page an on-call engineer if it notices a BGP neighbor of a core device going down.
- Kafka allows us to build a centralized pipeline for network data processing instead of having dispersed teams process bits and pieces of data separately.

These are just some of the use cases of Kafka. By the end of this book, I am sure we will be able to find much more creative use cases.

Prerequisites for this book

Basic knowledge of Linux command line is required to make the most out of this book. We would use command-line tools such as using `cd` for changing directories, `ls` for listing directories contents, and `pwd` to know where in the directory tree you are currently operating from.

We will be using Python 3 as the programming language in this book. Python is a popular language amongst network engineers with a large ecosystem of tools and libraries. We will use Python to create Kafka producers, consumers and interface with public cloud providers. However, I do not believe you need to be an expert in Python 3 to understand the scripts in this book. If you need a refresher on Python, a good place to go would be the official Python Tutorial[2].

Who this book is for

This book is ideal for IT professionals and engineers who want to take advantage of Kafka's distributed, fault-tolerant streaming data platform. This book can also be used by management to gain a general understanding of Kafka and how it fits into the general IT infrastructure.

What this book covers

Chapter 1. Kafka Introduction, In this chapter, we will cover the general concepts of Kafka. The core architecture, components, and tools. The idea behind Kafka, how it was built, and how the components can help maintain data streams at scale.

Chapter 2. Kafka Installation and Testing, In this chapter, we will install Zookeeper and Kafka on a single Virtual Machine and configure both components. We will also prepare our network lab to be used for future

[2]https://docs.python.org/3/tutorial/

examples. After installation, we will work on a few producer-consumer examples using Kafka command-line tools.

Chapter 3. Kafka Concepts and Examples, In this chapter, we will provide examples of Kafka usage for Producers and Consumers. The producers will write messages to a Topic with consumers receiving the messages. We will look at examples of offset, commit, and acknowledgment for data in the topics.

Chapter 4. Hosted Kafka Services, When we want to move Kafka from our lab setup into production, we can use the Kafka-hosting-as-a-service provided by various cloud providers, such as Amazon AWS or Confluent Cloud. In this chapter, we will provide a step-by-step guide to launch our Kafka cluster using Amazon Managed Streaming for Apache Kafka.

Chapter 5. Cloud Providers Messaging Services, If we are not ready for a managed Kafka cluster, the top public cloud providers, Amazon AWS, Microsoft Azure, and Google Cloud, offer their adopted version of message streaming service. The messaging services have various degrees of Kafka compatibility. In this chapter, we will look at examples of AWS Kinesis, Azure Event Hub, and Google Pub/Sub.

Chapter 6. Network Operations with Kafka, In this chapter, we will explore examples of Kafka in network engineering. We will look at data feeds, data enhancement, and Kafka Connect. The Kafka Connect reuses code provided by the community. We will look at the File and Elasticsearch Kafka connect plugins.

Chapter 7. Other Kafka Considerations and Looking Ahead, In this chapter, we will discuss other Kafka considerations, such as hardware requirements, Broker and Topic configuration, Schema registry, and many more. This chapter will provide additional resources for readers to explore Kafka.

Download the example code files

The code examples used in this book can be downloaded from GitHub at https://github.com/ericchou1/network-devops-kafka-up-and-running[3].

Conventions used

There are a number of text conventions used in this book to help organize the flow. Information in **bold** and *italic* are used to indicate important or special terms.

Code blocks are shown below:

```
print('hello world')
```

Command-line input or output will be shown as follows:

```
$ touch my_script.py

$ ls /
bin    cdrom  etc   lib    lib64   lost+found  mnt  proc  run   snap  sw\
apfile  tmp   var
boot   dev    home  lib32  libx32  media       opt  root  sbin  srv   sy\
s       usr

$ python
Python 3.8.10 (default, Jun  2 2021, 10:49:15)
[GCC 9.4.0] on linux
Type "help", "copyright", "credits" or "license" for more information
>>> print('hello world')
```

[3]https://github.com/ericchou1/network-devops-kafka-up-and-running

```
hello world
>>> exit()
```

Warning, tips, and information will be specified in their own special block:

This is a tip section. It will include useful tips and tricks in relation to the topic discussed at hand.

This is an information section. It will provide additional information to help you explore the topic further.

This is a warning blurb. Please pay special attention to this section when they appear, as they will contain important warnings.

Get in touch

Feedbacks from our readers is always welcome and appreciated. Please consider leaving a review on various platforms. They can really help others to discover the book.

All feedback can be submitted to:

book-feedback@networkautomationnerds.com.

Chapter 1. Kafka Introduction

As mentioned in the introduction section, Apache Kafka[4] is a *high-throughput, low-latency platform for handling real-time data feeds.*

At first glance, 'low-latency, high-throughput for real-time data feed' might not look much. After all, every open-source project and commercial vendor (and their brother) can claim to be *low-latency* and *high-throughput.* But once you consider the *type* of companies using Kafka in their products and services, such as Uber, Netflix, LinkedIn, you quickly realize how significant that claim is. When we click on the *like* button on a LinkedIn post, it needs to appear on the post right away. That is low-latency. If we consider how many Netflix movies are streaming every second, that is high throughput. Of course, the customers of these companies expect all of the operations to take place in real-time.

According to Netflix, Kafka Inside Keystone Pipeline[5], "700 Billion messages are ingested on an average day" by their 400+ Kafka brokers. Did they say they process **700 Billion** messages in a day in real-time? Or let's also consider Uber's use case, Real-Time Exactly-Once Ad Event Processing[6], of being a two-way marketplace for UberEats. In it, the message needs to be fast and reliable, but they also need to ensure the events are processed only once, with no overcount or undercount. The events need to be **exactly** once amongst all the consumers, full stop.

[4] https://en.wikipedia.org/wiki/Apache_Kafka

[5] https://netflixtechblog.com/kafka-inside-keystone-pipeline-dd5aeabaf6bb

[6] https://eng.uber.com/real-time-exactly-once-ad-event-processing/

Kafka is excellent at how it can achieve its goals for these demanding projects. But how did this fantastic tool come about? First, let's look into the history of Kafka.

History of Kafka

Kafka was originally developed at LinkedIn by Jay Kreps, Neha Narkhede, and Jun Rao (Wikipedia)[7]. As the story goes, Jay Kreps named the project Kafka because he likes the author Franz Kafka's work. The author Franze Kafa has a 'system optimized for writing' and Apache Kafka is also "a system optimzed for writing"[8].

The project was released as an open-sourced project with the Apache Software Foundation in early 2011 and went from incubation to top-level apache project on October 23, 2012. It is written in Java and Scala with significant community backing.

The three original developers left LinkedIn and found the company Confluent[9] in 2014. The company aims to *Set Data in Motion* with (surprise!) Kafka is at the center of that idea. As a result, many of the Kafka-related projects, documentation, products, and initiatives are actively developed and sponsored by Confluent.

Kafka Use Cases

Within the Kafka architecture, at the center is the idea of **event streaming**. Software systems drive our world. These systems are *interconnected,*

[7] https://en.wikipedia.org/wiki/Apache_Kafka

[8] https://events19.linuxfoundation.org/wp-content/uploads/2017/12/Apache-Kafka_Bernhard-H_oss_2018.pdf

[9] https://www.confluent.io/about

always-on, and automated. Kafka provides the centralized middle ground for these systems to exchange information, or events, in the form of *topics* (or categories). The producer systems can send events to a particular topic, while the consumer systems can receive these events via subscription.

> We will use the term *events* and *messages* interchangeably in this book to refer to the data being exchanged by producers, consumers, and Kafka.

In the words of Kafka, event streaming is analogous to the central nervous system of the human body, which allows the connectivity of tissues between different parts of the body.

In terms of network engineering, in my opinion, can use Kafka event streaming in a few different scenarios:

- We can use Kafka to process transactions in real-time, such as device provisioning from warehouse shipment to fully functional in a data center.
- We can use Kafka to implement an event-driven architecture. Kafka can be used to track and analyze changes in network events, such as BGP neighbor relationships or interface flapping.
- We can use Kafka to capture and analyze IoT and wireless sensor data continuously. This process can be done in a distributed fashion, with Kafka servers across different regions.
- We can use Kafka to connect, store, and make available data produced by a *single* source to multiple destinations. An example would be to store a single set of network SNMP data in a Kafka topic, which multiple monitoring systems can consume. This allows us only to poll the network device once and reduce CPU and network overhead.

If we combine the above use cases, Kafka allows us to:

- Continuously capture events
- Connect different parts of the system
- Immediate react to a change in system state
- Minimizing the impact on the network devices

We will look at some of the disadvantages of Kafka in the next section.

Disadvantages of Kafka

If Kafka is so great, why doesn't everybody use Kafka? Of course, no system can be perfect. Like many, if not all, system design approaches, the design of Kafka is a story of tradeoffs. What are some of the disadvantages of Kafka? Let's take a look at a few of them:

- Kafka clusters can be complex and hard to set up.
- Managing a Kafka can have a high learning curve.
- By design, Kafka does not contain some standard features found in other storage solutions. For example, Kafka does not by default have message validation for producers.
- Kaka has a fast, evolving ecosystem that sometimes makes keeping systems up-to-date a challenge.

Even with the foretold disadvantages, in my opinion, the benefits of Kafka still outweigh the disadvantages. Let us take a look at some of the key concepts in Kafka.

Kafka Concepts

Kafka was developed with the newer data pipeline in mind, which treats data as a continuous stream. As a result, there are several parts and concepts related to the Kafka data streaming system:

1. In a distributed system, we need a way to *build*, *manage*, *scaling*, and *maintain* the group of distributed servers. The Kafka system uses **Zookeepers**, another open-source project, to manage the servers within the cluster. The Kafka servers containing the data themselves (Topics and events) are called **Brokers**.
2. The system allows for *producing* (write) and *subscribing* (read) the messages continuously. Hence, they are appropriately named **Producers** and **Consumers**. The producers and consumers generally take the form of SDK or APIs sitting in the servers communicating to the Kafka cluster. In this book, we will use the Python SDK and shell scripts as producers and consumers.
3. The system needs to *store* the events for some time. This step is generally in the form of **Topics** consisting of **Partitions**. Within the partitions, each event is labeled with a number called **offset**. This is the identification of the message we use to keep track of which the consumers have consumed.
4. The systems need to **process** the streams of events as they occur and react to any unforeseen circumstances, such as backing up partitions and reallocating them when a Broker is unexpectedly down. The components responsible for these processes are Zookeepers and Brokers.

Here is a generalized overview of the Kafka cluster from Wikipedia[10]:

[10]https://upload.wikimedia.org/wikipedia/commons/6/64/Overview_of_Apache_Kafka.svg

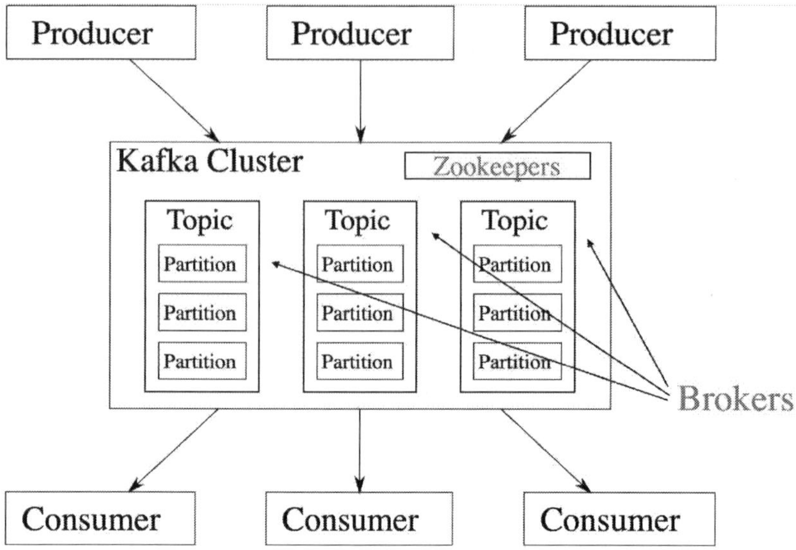

Figure 1.1 Kafka Overview

We will go over the components in more detail. Let's start with Zookeepers.

Zookeepers

Apache Zookeepers is in itself a popular open-source project under the Apache Software Foundation. Its primary function is to provide reliable distributed coordination between applications. Why is the project named Zookeeper, you asked? The project received its funny name because it started as a sub-project of Hadoop. Since many of the projects in Hadoop are named after zoo animals, Zookeeper received its name for its management function. What started as a Hadoop sub-project is now a top-level Apache project (at least in 2019) in its own right.

There can be multiple Zookeepers in a Kafka cluster, and the recommended number is three to five Zookeepers in a production Kafka cluster.

The number should be an odd number to keep a quorum for leader election. However, the number should be kept as low as possible to minimize the overhead.

> For more information on Zookeeper, please see Apache Zookeeper[11].

It is important to realize Zookeeper is a separate service with its configuration file and run time service for our purpose. It is also important to note that Kafka brokers require Zookeepers to function *prior* to be put into service. The Zookeeper keeps the state of the cluster, such as Brokers, Topics, users, and more.

Brokers

The Kafka Brokers are the workhorse of the Kafka cluster. Generally, *a single Kafka server is one broker.* We will see how we can run multiple brokers in a single machine later in the book, but that is more of a hack than an actual setup we would use in production. There has to be at least one Broker per Kafka cluster. Each broker has a broker ID that it uses to register with Zookeeper.

Kafka broker is where the producers and clients will communicate with the cluster when they need to write or read messages from a topic. They handle most of the requests from clients. The broker receives messages from producers, assigns offsets to them, and commits them to storage on disk. At this point, the broker would send a confirmation to the producer to signal the success of the message commit. The broker also services consumers. They would respond to message pull requests from the consumer.

[11] https://en.wikipedia.org/wiki/Apache_ZooKeeper

Depending on the hardware, one broker can handle thousands of requests. We will have at least one broker per cluster, but having more than one broker allows redundancy and additional performance gain. Kafka brokers are designed to be operated as part of a cluster. Within a cluster, one broker will be elected as the *controller*. The controller is responsible for assigning partitions to brokers and monitoring other broker failures.

As we will see in the next section on Topics and Partitions, when we have multiple brokers, the same topic can be distributed into different partitions. A *leader* is elected in a partition to service messages. The partitions can also be assigned to multiple brokers, which can serve as replication for redundancy. The clients can have concurrent connections to multiple brokers for scalability.

> Don't worry too much about leaders and controllers between Kafka brokers at this point. For now, it is enough to know they exist and their general functions. The leadership election happens automatically within the cluster.

We have talked about Kafka messages can be retained on the Kafka cluster for some time. Once committed by the broker, the message by default is kept on the disk for seven days or when the topic reaches a certain size, 1 GB by default. Both of these parameters are configurable options on the broker. With the message being retained on the broker for a while, the consumers can be down for a bit of time before the message is deleted.

Topics, Partitions, and Offsets

A *topic* is simply a category or name of a feed. We can configure our cluster to allow automatic topic creation when the sender feeds our cluster a topic that does not exist. A good analogy for a topic would be a file folder on your computer. Just like we group related files into a folder, we group related messages into a topic.

Kafka's topics are divided into several partitions. The multiple partitions per topic allow data to be split across multiple brokers. Having the message across numerous brokers allows parallel processing. When we want to increase the read-write performance, one of the options is to increase the number of brokers and partitions for our topics.

In the Figure below, we can see Topic A was divided into two partitions, and each partition has a replication factor of 2 for redundancy. The placement of the partitions are intelligently managed by Zookeeper between the three brokers:

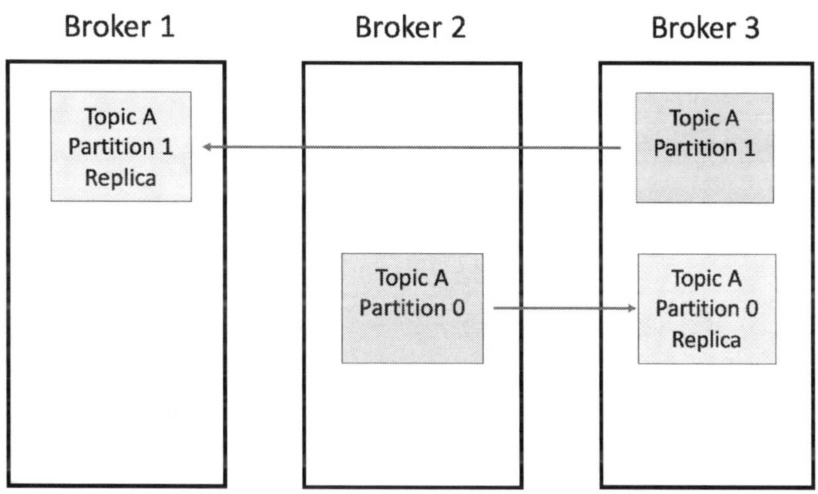

Figure 1.2 Kafka Topics and Partitions

Each of the partitions will contain the actual messages in an orderly fashion. The messages are immutable, meaning they cannot be changed once written to the partition. The messages are written to a partition in an append-only manner. Once the message is written to a partition, the broker will commit the message with a commit log. Please note that as each topic will likely have multiple partitions, the ordering of messages across the topic would not be guaranteed. However, if we have a key in the message, Kafka will put the message in the same partition, and the message ordering within that partition is guaranteed. We will see this in an example in the next chapter.

Each of the messages in the partition is assigned a number called *offset*:

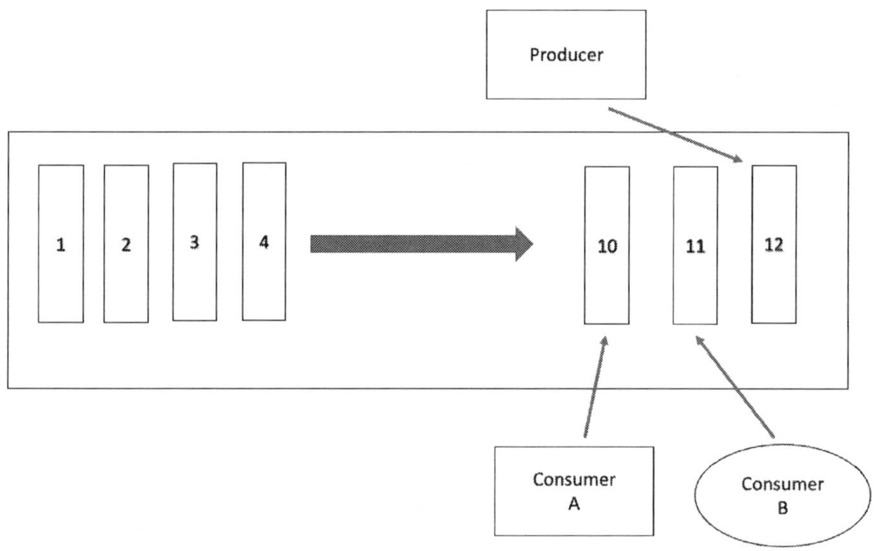

Figure 1.3 Message Offsets

The concept of offset is essential; this offset number gives a point of reference in the messages. It allows the Zookeeper to know when a producer sends a new message to an existing topic, where it should append a new message. The offset also allows the Kafka cluster to keep track of where the consumer has processed the messages. This tracking stays active even when the consumers join together to form a consumer group. For example, in Figure 1.3, Consumer A has processed up to message offset 10, whereas Consumer B has processed the message offset 11. Assuming Consumer A and B are in different groups, the following message to Consumer A should be 11, whereas the following message to Consumer B should be 12.

In the last section, we mentioned a broker is elected as the leader. Every partition and replica group has one server acting as the leader who will handle all read-write options while the rest of the replicas copy its leader's messages. If a leader fails, one of the followers will be elected as the new leader.

It is worth repeating that the messages with the same key will be put into the same partition. This is convenient to us as we would be sure that all the message for the same key is kept in the order Kafka received them. For example, we can have a topic of BGP with each message produced containing a key of the router ID. These messages will be kept in the order they were written to the Kafka broker; this is a Kafka guarantee. When we consume these messages, we know the messages with the same router ID will be in the same petition and the order it was written. Thus, the consumer will receive the messages in the same first-in-first-out order.

Producers and Consumers

The *producers* and *consumers* are applications writing to and reading from the Kafka cluster. When the producer sends a message to a topic, it is published to the topic partition's leader. The leader will commit the message to its log and increment the record offset. Kafka will only send the message to the consumer once the message is committed. Therefore, we can configure our producer to wait for the message commit confirmation. If confirmation is not received, the producer can resend the message to ensure the integrity of message delivery.

Since the producer needs to write to the leader in the partition, in a cluster, how does it know which broker contains the leader for the partition? Before the producer can send any message, it has to request metadata about the cluster from the broker. The metadata contains information on which broker the producer should write to. Althought this might sound complicated; luckily, if we use a Kafka producer SDK, this exchange is usually taken care of for us.

Consumers pull messages from the topic specified to Kafka. To be precise, the messages are from the broker which contains the partitions of the messages. In practice, consumers typically form *consumer groups*. A consumer group is a group of consumers who share the same group ID. They allow multiple consumers to share the load of process messages.

When consumers want to read a message from a topic, they can choose to read from the beginning or from a particular committed offset. For example, when a new consumer group is initially constructed, the consumers can choose to read all the messages from the beginning. However, when a new member joins an existing consumer group, it will probably only read from the uncommitted or new messages published on that topic. For example, imagine a group of credit card processing consumers, when they start, they would want to 'clear out' all the backlogs of unprocessed transactions. Once that is done, they would want to process newly created transactions. The load balance of messages across consumers in a consumer group is handled automatically by Kafka.

Consumer groups are a great way to parallelize operations; multiple consumers can process the messages simultaneously. As mentioned, the best part is that this load balancing of messages is automatically taken care of by Kafka. Due to the benefit of consumer groups, even if we only have one consumer, we typically launch it with a consumer group. In the future, more consumers can join the group if need be.

Other Elements in the Ecosystem

We have briefly covered the core concepts and components of Kafka in this chapter. However, Kafka is a very popular project that has a fast-evolving ecosystem. Below is a partial list of tools that integrates with the main distribution.

- Kafka Connect: Kafka connect is a built-in framework of *connectors*. These connectors allow us to use pre-build code for different sources and different destinations called sinks. For example, connector sources for relational databases and destination sinks for Elastic-search, Amazon S3, and Azure Blob Storage. We will see examples of Kafka connect in chapter 6.
- Stream Processing: If we treat data as a continuous stream, it will make sense to have multiple steps in the streaming process. The toolchain in the Kafka stream is vast enough to have dedicated projects and libraries. There are many complex stream processing libraries for the Kafka project, such as Kafka Streams, Storm, Samza, Kafka-Storm, etc.
- Management Consoles: There are many projects related to the management of Kafka, such as Kafka Manager, Kafkat, Cruise Controle, etc.

Take a look at the Kafka Connectors List[12] maintained by Confluent to see the list of common connectors available.

As we are only learning about Kafka, we do not need to go in-depth about the ecosystem of Kafka. In my opinion, Kafka connect is the most important project outside of core Kafka components. I would recommend taking a look at the list of connectors to be aware of their existence.

[12] https://docs.confluent.io/home/connect/kafka_connectors.html

Conclusion

In this chapter, we briefly looked at the history of Kafka, its advantages and disadvantages, the main concepts, and the ecosystem. We learned about Zookeepers, brokers, producers, consumers, topics, partitions, and offsets. Even at a high level, there are many important components that we need to know before moving on.

Kafka is a complex system to learn, and this chapter can be a bit confusing at first. This chapter is the most concept-heavy chapter in the book. Starting in the next chapter, we will begin to work with hands-on examples. We will begin by installing a lab instance. It will allow us to start working with Kafka examples and help us understand the Kafka concepts better.

Chapter 2. Kafka Installation and Testing

In chapter 1, we learned about the basic operations and concepts of Kafka. In this chapter, we will install our first Kafka cluster, configure the cluster with necessary components, work with the Kafka console command-line interface, and set up the server so Kafka can start as a system service.

Depending on your budget and environment, there are many ways we can spin up a Kafka cluster. The cluster can be as small as a single instance or as big as a full-blown, production-ready cluster with multiple dedicated instances of redundant Zookeepers with hundreds of brokers.

We will launch a new instance of virtual machine for our lab and install both Zookeeper and Broker on the same machine. Having only one device to manage will allow us to step into the operation quickly without getting too bogged down on the various configuration options (Hint. it can get pretty complicated). But having just one instance will impose some limitations, such as partitions. We will point out the minor differences when we encounter them.

When I say configuration options can be complicated, it *can* get pretty hairy. There are over 140+ configuration options in the Kafka Broker configuration file alone. So, for now, let's just stick with a single host.

The base operating system will be Ubuntu 20.04 LTS, and this is a long-term support version of Ubuntu. The official support is for five years from the release date. For installation on other operating systems such as Mac, Windows, and different flavors of Linux, please consult the Kafka Documentation[13] and other resources.

Digital Ocean[14] has a great Kafka installation tutorial. On the page, you can find a drop-down menu to pick different operating systems.

What about containers and Kubernetes? On the surface, Kafka and Kubernetes might look like a perfect fit. But my personal experience is that they are not very straightforward at this time. The same reason you do not see a lot of databases run in containers is the same reason you do not see a lot of production Kafka clusters using containers. We will, however, use containers for some of our examples in Chapter 6.

Let us take a look at the network lab in the next section.

Network Lab Setup

Since we are all 'networking' guys and gals, my assumption is we all have some type of network lab consisting of network gears. In this book, we will use the network lab gears to demonstrate how they can work with Kafka. Do not worry if you do not have the 'exact' same topology, device count, or software version that I listed below. As we will see later, the example we will use does not require all the devices in the lab. Therefore, you should be able to replicate the examples we will use with just a subset of devices running different software versions.

[13]https://kafka.apache.org/documentation/

[14]https://www.digitalocean.com/community/tutorials/how-to-install-apache-kafka-on-ubuntu-20-04

I am using Cisco CML2 for my lab. The topology file is included in the course GitHub repository on https://github.com/ericchou1/network-devops-kafka-up-and-running[15]:

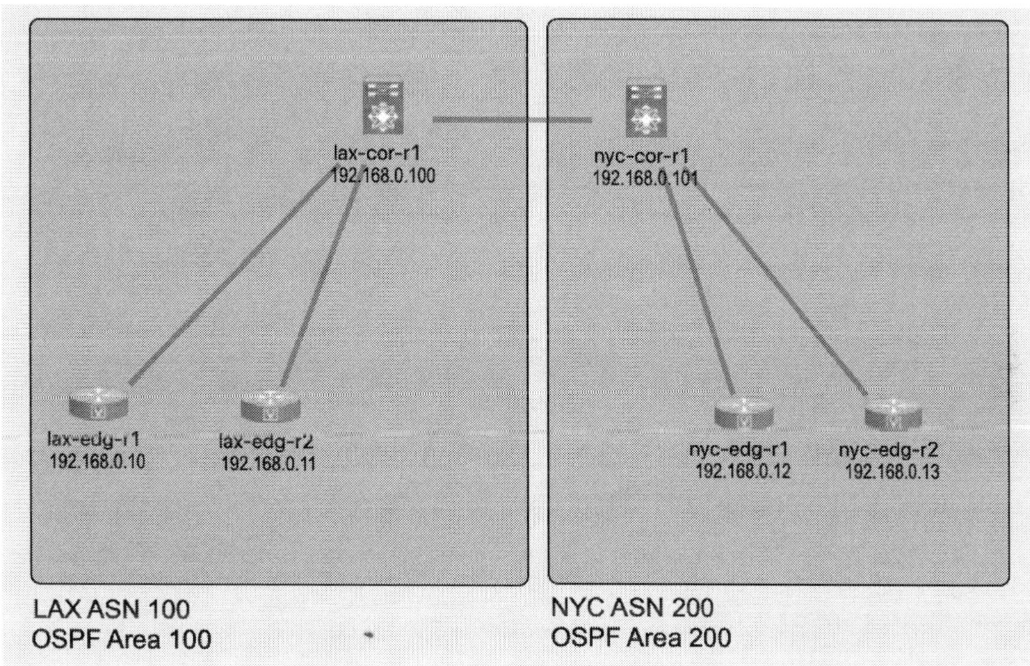

Figure 2.1 Network Lab Topology

Here is what the CML2 lab consists of:

- 2 virtual Data Centers, LAX and NYC.
- eBGP between the two Data Centers.
- iBGP inside of each Data Centers, with the core devices being the route reflector.
- OSPF as IGP.
- The Core switches are Cisco Nexus devices.
- The Edge switches are Cisco IOS devices.

[15]https://github.com/ericchou1/network-devops-kafka-up-and-running

The P2P interface IPs are not that important, as they only provide connectivity. The management IP and Loopback IP are more relevant to us. We use the management IPs for connectivity, and the loopback IPs are used for BGP neighborship establishment.

The device Loopback and management IPs are listed below:

Device	Loopback	Management	BGP ASN
lax-cor-r1	192.168.0.100	192.168.2.50	100
lax-edg-r1	192.168.0.10	192.168.2.51	100
lax-edg-r2	192.168.0.11	192.168.2.52	100
nyc-cor-r1	192.168.0.101	192.168.2.60	200
nyc-edg-r1	192.168.0.12	192.168.2.61	200
nyc-edg-r2	192.168.0.13	192.168.2.62	200

All devices have the user *cisco* with password *cisco* configured. The user also has administrative privileges:

```
nyc-edg-r1#sh run
...
username cisco privilege 15 secret 5 $1$nMo.$UborfI9yTGPnN8926xJY/.
...
line vty 0 4
 exec-timeout 720 0
 password cisco
 login local
 transport input telnet ssh
!
```

In the next section, we will install our much anticipated Kafka cluster. In our initial setup, we will install Zookeeper and Kafka on the same host. We will only have one broker in this lab cluster. It will be a minimal but functional Apache Kafka cluster.

Kafka Installation Overview

Here are the general installation steps we will follow:

1. Install Java8.
2. Download Kafka all-in-one pacakge.
3. Configure Zookeeper.
4. Configure Kafka.
5. Start Zookeeper and Kafka manually.
6. Test the Kafka operation with console tools.
7. Configure system services to include Zookeeper and Kafka services.

Just as a reminder, if this is a brand new install of Ubuntu, we should update the repository list as well as upgrade the default packages:

```
$ sudo apt update && sudo apt -y upgrade
```

Ready? Let's go.

Install Java

Kafka is written in Java and Scala. Its native API is Java. Therefore, we will need to install Java before we can run Kafka. There are a few different versions of Java, and we will install the free and open-source implementation of the *openjdk-8-jdk* edition:

```
$ sudo apt install openjdk-8-jdk
```

> Being one of the older and mature cross-platform programming languages, Java has a long and interesting versioning story. Take a look at Java version history Wikipedia page[16] for more information.

The installation should take a minute to complete, verify the Java version after installation:

```
$ java -version
openjdk version "1.8.0_292"
OpenJDK Runtime Environment (build 1.8.0_292-8u292-b10-0ubuntu1~20.04-b\
10)
OpenJDK 64-Bit Server VM (build 25.292-b10, mixed mode)
```

Once Java is installed. We can move on to install the Kafka all-in-one binary.

Download Kafka

Please consult the Apache Kafka page[17] for the latest version of Kafka. We should download the binary build and not the source code:

[16] https://en.wikipedia.org/wiki/Java_version_history
[17] https://kafka.apache.org/downloads

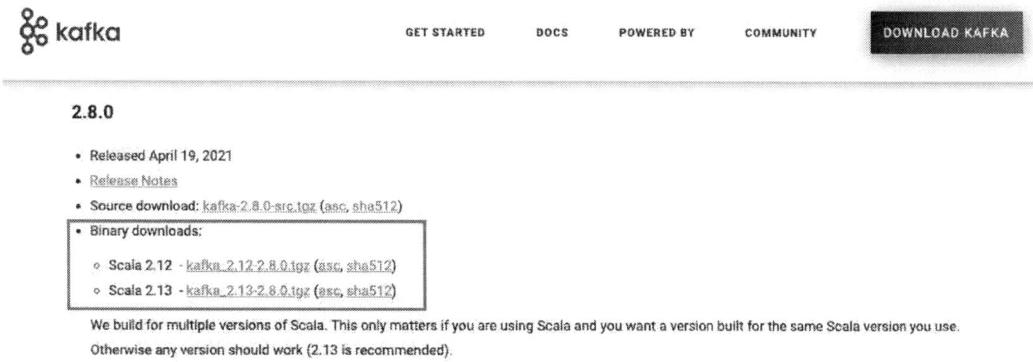

Figure 2.2 Kafka Binary Download

We can use curl to download the binary image directly to our home directory:

The ~ sign below indicates the home directory, in my case, */home/echou.*

```
$ cd ~
$ curl -O "https://archive.apache.org/dist/kafka/2.8.0/kafka_2.13-2.8.0\
.tgz"
```

Unzip and untar the file:

```
$ tar -xvzf kafka_2.13-2.8.0.tgz
```

We now have the Kafka folder in our home directory. The Kafka directory contains the */config* and */bin* directories. The */config* contains the sample configuration files for Kafka, Zookeeper, Connector, and many more. The */bin* directory contains many of the useful shell scripts. We can use these scripts to start and stop the Zookeeper process and Kafka brokers, as well as many other functions. The */bin* directory is where we will find the Kafka console CLI that we will use to test our setup.

```
$ ls ~/kafka_2.13-2.8.0/config/ kafka_2.13-2.8.0/bin/
kafka_2.13-2.8.0/bin/:
connect-distributed.sh          kafka-preferred-replica-election.sh
connect-mirror-maker.sh         kafka-producer-perf-test.sh
connect-standalone.sh           kafka-reassign-partitions.sh
kafka-acls.sh                   kafka-replica-verification.sh
kafka-broker-api-versions.sh    kafka-run-class.sh
kafka-cluster.sh                kafka-server-start.sh
kafka-configs.sh                kafka-server-stop.sh
kafka-console-consumer.sh       kafka-storage.sh
kafka-console-producer.sh       kafka-streams-application-reset.sh
kafka-consumer-groups.sh        kafka-topics.sh
kafka-consumer-perf-test.sh     kafka-verifiable-consumer.sh
kafka-delegation-tokens.sh      kafka-verifiable-producer.sh
kafka-delete-records.sh         trogdor.sh
kafka-dump-log.sh               windows
kafka-features.sh               zookeeper-security-migration.sh
kafka-leader-election.sh        zookeeper-server-start.sh
kafka-log-dirs.sh               zookeeper-server-stop.sh
kafka-metadata-shell.sh         zookeeper-shell.sh
kafka-mirror-maker.sh

kafka_2.13-2.8.0/config/:
connect-console-sink.properties     consumer.properties
connect-console-source.properties   kraft
connect-distributed.properties      log4j.properties
connect-file-sink.properties        producer.properties
connect-file-source.properties      server.properties
connect-log4j.properties            tools-log4j.properties
connect-mirror-maker.properties     trogdor.conf
connect-standalone.properties       zookeeper.properties
```

Since we will be using the commands inside of the bin directory frequently, I recommend adding this directory it to our path. On Linux Bash shells, this can be done by adding the following directory to the bottom of my ~/**.bashrc** file:

> Remember to switch the '/home/echou' directory in the example below with your own username for your home directory. You will also need to log out and log back into the terminal for this setting to take effect.

```
export PATH=/home/echou/kafka_2.13-2.8.0/bin:$PATH
```

> If you do not add the bin directory to your path, you will have to remember to type out the whole path, e.g. */home/echou/kafka_-2.13-2.8.0/bin*, every time you need to use the shell scripts.

If you recall, Kafka brokers are managed by Zookeepers. Therefore, we will need to configure and initiate Zookeeper before we can start our Kafka brokers. Configure Zookeeper is what we will do in the next section.

Configure Zookeeper

The *config/zookeeper.properties* file is what we will use to configure the zookeeper properties:

```
$ ls ~/kafka_2.12-2.8.1/config/zookeeper.properties
kafka_2.12-2.8.1/config/zookeeper.properties
```

Most of the management data by Kafka, such as commit logs and offset logs, are simple files written to the disk. Let's create a directory called *data* inside of the Kafka directory. This is where we will put Zookeeper and Kafka output files:

```
$ mkdir ~/kafka_2.13-2.8.0/data
```

There are many configuration options for Zookeeper. For now, we will only need to change the *log.dirs* option. Use your favorite text editor to change the following field in the *~/kafka_2.13-2.8.0/config/zookeeper.properties* file:

> Remember /home/echou is my home directory. In your setup, you should use your own home directory path.

```
dataDir=/home/echou/kafka_2.13-2.8.0/data/zookeeper
```

This will direct all the Zookeeper outputs, such as log commits, to the new directory.

Configure Kafka

We will use the *~/kafka_2.13-2.8.0/config/server.properties* file to configure our Kafka broker. Similar to the Zookeeper configuration, we will leave everything else as default and change the *logs.dir* directory to the one we created:

> Again, remember */home/echou* is my home directory. You should use your own home directory path in the configuration.

```
log.dirs=/home/echou/kafka_2.13-2.8.0/data/kafka
```

We can also optionally change the number of partitions from 1 to 3. For the most part, I prefer to manually specify the number of partitions when the topic is created. This setting will apply to topics that are automatically created. More partition allows better parallel data processing, so there is harm in changing this setting:

```
num.partitions=3
```

Now we are ready to start the Zookeeper and Kafka servers locally.

Start Zookper and Kafka manually

To begin testing, we will start the Zookeeper via a console command script in a terminal window:

> Remember /home/echou is my home directory, you should use your own home directory path.

> I am using the full path in the example for illustration. If you have added the *bin* directory to your path, you can use *zookeeper-server-start.sh* directly.

```
$ /home/echou/kafka_2.13-2.8.0/bin/zookeeper-server-start.sh /home/echo\
u/kafka_2.13-2.8.0/config/zookeeper.properties
```

We will see a bunch of startup messages scrolling over the screen. Eventually, things will be settled, and we will see the Zookeeper server running on the default port 2181:

```
[2021-08-23 19:09:04,887] INFO Reading configuration from: config/zooke\
eper.properties (org.apache.zookeeper.server.quorum.QuorumPeerConfig)
[2021-08-23 19:09:04,891] WARN config/zookeeper.properties is relative.\
 Prepend ./ to indicate that you're sure! (org.apache.zookeeper.server.\
quorum.QuorumPeerConfig)
[2021-08-23 19:09:04,901] INFO clientPortAddress is 0.0.0.0:2181 (org.a\
pache.zookeeper.server.quorum.QuorumPeerConfig)
```

At this point, we can open another terminal window to start the Kafka Broker (remember to use your home directory path):

```
$ /home/echou/kafka_2.13-2.8.0/bin/kafka-server-start.sh /home/echou/ka\
fka_2.13-2.8.0/config/server.properties
```

We will see the startup messages for Kafka, and eventually, we will see Kafka starts to run on default port 9092:

```
[2021-08-23 19:20:11,037] INFO [KafkaServer id=0] started (kafka.server\
.KafkaServer)
[2021-08-24 17:31:58,085] INFO Awaiting socket connections on 0.0.0.0:9\
092. (kafka.network.Acceptor)
```

Let's leave the two terminals running and open up two more terminal windows. One terminal will be used to produce messages, and the other terminal will be used to receive messages. If your terminal program supports it, it would be great to place these two windows side-by-side. We can see the messages between producers and consumers in real-time.

Test the Kafka operations

In the first terminal window for producers, we will create a topic called 'my_first_topic' with the Zookeeper using *kafka-topic.sh*:

> If you have not added the *bin* directory to your shell path, please use the full path for *kafka-topic.sh*. The command will need the required switches to specify Zookeeper, topic name, and action:

```
$ kafka-topics.sh --zookeeper 127.0.0.1:2181 --topic my_first_topic --c\
reate --partitions 3 --replication-factor 1
```

Note the number of partitions and replication-factor in our console command script. If we specify a replication factor greater than one, our command will fail. This is due to the fact that we only have one broker at this time. If we specify more than one replication, Kafka would have no other broker to put the extra partitions to.

After the topic is created, we can continue to use the first terminal window to start a consumer. The consumer can be started with *kafka-console-consumer.sh* to subscribe to the topic we created. We will specify the location of our broker with the *bootstra-server* option:

```
$ kafka-console-consumer.sh --bootstrap-server 127.0.0.1:9092 --topic m\
y_first_topic
```

The consumer shell will appear as if it is not doing anything with a blinking cursor. Don't worry, as soon as there are messages published to the topic, my_first_topic, we will see them on our consumer screen. Let us use the second terminal window we opened to produce messages. This is done with the *kafka-console-producer.sh* script. Please note we can use either *broker-list* or *bootstrap-server* to indicate the location of our broker:

> For older versions of Kafka, we need to use *broker-list*.

```
$ kafka-console-producer.sh --broker-list 127.0.0.1:9092 --topic my_fir\
st_topic
```

The command will return with a prompt, we can use this prompt to type in the messages we will send to the topic. As soon as we type in our messages from the producer terminal, we should see them appear on the consumer window.

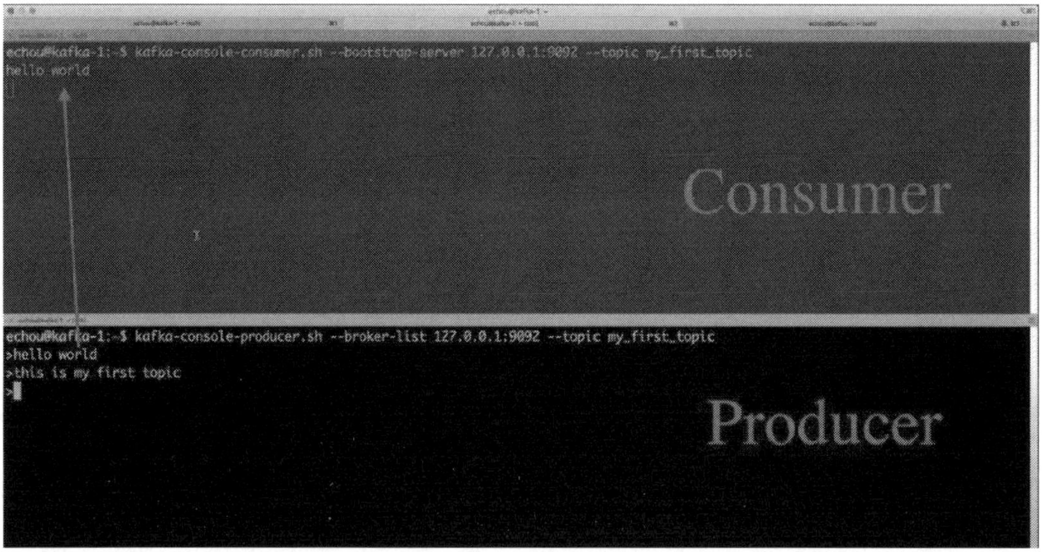

Figure 2.3 Producer and Consumer Console Testing

Is that cool or what? We just created our first Kafka topic, produced some messages, and received the messages from that topic! We can use *Ctrl+C* to exit out of all the processes.

Configure System Services

We can continue to manually start Zookeeper and brokers every time we reboot the server. While it is a great way to practice the commands, the process can become tedious pretty quickly. Ideally, we would start the services automatically. For Ubuntu 20.04 servers, this can be done using systemd[18].

Below is my unit file for Zookeeper (remember to replace '/home/echou' with your own user path):

```
$ cat /etc/systemd/system/zookeeper.service
[Unit]
Requires=network.target remote-fs.target
After=network.target remote-fs.target

[Service]
Type=simple
User=echou
ExecStart=/home/echou/kafka_2.13-2.8.0/bin/zookeeper-server-start.sh /h\
ome/echou/kafka_2.13-2.8.0/config/zookeeper.properties
ExecStop=/home/echou/kafka_2.13-2.8.0/bin/zookeeper-server-stop.sh
Restart=on-abnormal

[Install]
WantedBy=multi-user.target
```

Here is my unit file for Kafka (remember to replace '/home/echou' with your own user path):

[18] https://wiki.ubuntu.com/systemd

```
$ cat /etc/systemd/system/kafka.service
[Unit]
Requires=zookeeper.service
After=zookeeper.service

[Service]
Type=simple
User=echou
ExecStart=/bin/sh -c '/home/echou/kafka_2.13-2.8.0/bin/kafka-server-sta\
rt.sh /home/echou/kafka_2.13-2.8.0/config/server.properties > /home/ech\
ou/kafka_2.13-2.8.0/kafka.log 2>&1'
ExecStop=/home/echou/kafka_2.13-2.8.0/bin/kafka-server-stop.sh
Restart=on-abnormal

[Install]
WantedBy=multi-user.target
```

We will be able to start, stop, and check the status of our services:

```
$ sudo systemctl stop zookeeper
$ sudo systemctl start zookeeper
$ sudo systemctl status zookeeper
$ sudo systemctl stop kafka
$ sudo systemctl start kafka
$ sudo systemctl status kafka
```

We can add the services to start automatically when the server starts:

```
$ sudo systemctl enable zookeeper
$ sudo systemctl enable kafka
```

We now have a Kafka test cluster ready to go!

Conclusion

In this chapter, we went thru all the necessary steps to install a test Kafka cluster. We installed both Zookeeper and broker on the same server. Using the configuration files, we configure the data directories for both services. Then, we use the shell scripts to manually start the services.

With the services started, we use the console command scripts to create a topic, produce messages to the topic, and use console consumers to receive the messages. Once we ensure the services are running as expected, we use the Ubuntu systemd to add the two services to system control and automatically start them when the server starts.

In the next chapter, we will dive deeper into learning the core aspects of Kafka with examples.

Chapter 3. Kafka Concepts and Examples

In Chapter 2, we built a small but functional Kafka lab cluster consisting of one Zookeeper and one broker. In this chapter, we will use the lab cluster to learn more about Kafka with various examples.

Producers: Writing Messages

If we do not have any data that needs to be stored and passed on to other systems, there is no need for Kafka or any messaging system, right? So it makes sense to start our learning journey with producers. Producers are systems responsible for writing data to Kafka. Writing data might sound easy, but as they say, the devil is always in the details. From the perspective of Kafka, the system would need to keep track of message receipts, makes redundant copies, and send confirmation back to the sender. All of these steps would need to be completed on a per-topic basis.

There are also other business restrictions, such as message latency requirements and load balancing the storage load. For example, if we use Kafka to track device deployment steps, the producers of messages probably have less strict requirements than if we use it to alert BGP neighbor down events.

When we create a producer, it has several important jobs. At the top level, we will create a record consist of a topic, optional key, and value.

Even though a key in the record is optional, often, we would include a key. We will explain more about message keys later in the chapter. For now, just remember: **Kafka will put all the records with the same key in the same partition. Apache Kakfa will also preserve the order of messages within a partition as they were written to the parition**. The orders has implications on the ordering of messages when they are received on the consumer end.

After the record is created, the producer will serialize the object into ByteArrays. This step is required for the messages to be sent over the network. Next, the producer will determine a partition to send the message to. If the record does not contain a key (value of null), the record will be sent to a partition at random. However, if the record contains a key, the partition will be based on the hashed value of the key.

The producer will then add the record to a batch of records of the same topic and partition. The batch will be sent after a certain size has been reached. This batching process makes delivery more efficient.

This is a generalization of the steps producers take to produce messages. There are a few details that we did not cover here, such as how to specify the partition in the record manually.

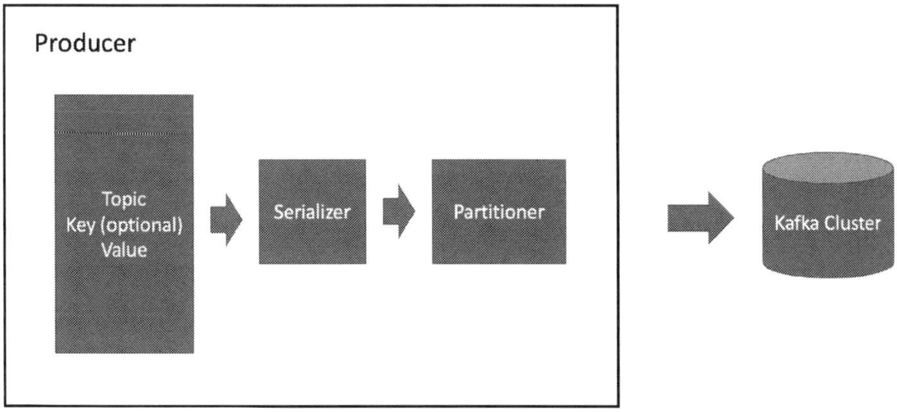

Figure 3.1 Kafka Producer

When the Kafka broker receives the message, it will send back a response for acknowledgment. The response will contain the topic and partition of the message. It will also include the offset number of the record (remember, the offset is a number that indicates the placement of the record). If there are replication factors for the partition, we can configure the broker only to send this acknowledgment when the replicas were made to ensure redundancy.

In the producer example from Chapter 2, we did not capture this confirmation from the Kafka broker. If we wanted to make sure the message was accurately received by the broker, we should have captured the acknowledgment. This acknowledgment is important for the producer to know if the message was accurately received by the Kafka broker. If not, the producer should retransmit the message.

There are three primary methods of sending messages:

- Fire-and-forget: The message is sent to the Kafka broker, and we do not care if it was successfully received. This was the method used in Chapter 2's example.

- Synchronous send: The producer will wait for the acknowledgment before it moves on to the next step. The process is blocked until the acknowledgment is received.
- Asynchronous send: We will send the message along with a callback function. The broker will use this callback function to let the producer know when the message is received. We will see examples of asynchronous send in this chapter.

For our next example, let's use the *kafka-topic.sh* command to create a new topic, ch3_topic_1:

```
$ kafka-topics.sh --zookeeper 127.0.0.1:2181 --topic ch3_topic_1 --crea\
te --partitions 3 --replication-factor 1

Created topic ch3_topic_1.
```

Creating a new topic is technically an optional step. By default, the *auto.create.topics.enable* option in Zookeeper configuration is set to true. Therefore, if we start sending a message from a producer to a new topic that does not exist, the topic will be automatically created. However, I feel it is better to create the topic manually when we are just learning about Kafka. In production, you may wish to turn off *auto.create.topic.enable* to keep tighter control over topic creation.

Producer Example

Let's start a console consumer on a new terminal window to watch for new messages on this topic. Just like what we did in Chapter 2, we will leave the consumer running to observe the result in real-time:

```
$ kafka-console-consumer.sh --bootstrap-server 127.0.0.1:9092 --topic c\
h3_topic_1 --property print.key=true --property key.separator=,
```

For readers with a sharp eye, they might notice this console consumer command is a little different than the one we used in Chapter 2. It added the option *print.key=true* to print the keys in the messages. The *key.separater=,* tells the consumer the comma is the separator between the key and the value.

To write messages to the topic, we will use Confluent's Python client[19]. The confluent-kafka documentation[20] is a helpful resource to read on the different options on the Python client.

As with any modern Python application, we will start by creating a Python 3 virtual environment. Python virtual environment is typically used to separate the individual Python environments from the operating system's Python installation.

```
$ sudo apt install python3-pip
$ sudo apt install python3-venv
$ python3 -m venv venv
$ source venv/bin/activate
```

> From this point on, I will skip the above steps and assume the virtual environment is active.

We will install the necessary libraries in this virtual environment:

```
$ pip install requests certifi confluent-kafka[avro,json,protobuf]
```

For convenience, we will also add *kafka-1* to our host file:

[19] https://github.com/confluentinc/confluent-kafka-python
[20] https://docs.confluent.io/platform/current/clients/confluent-kafka-python/html/index.html

```
$ cat /etc/hosts | grep kafka-1
127.0.1.1       kafka-1
```

The first script we will use, creatively named *ch3_producer_1.py*, is pretty straightforward. Here is an overiew of the steps in the script:

- We will import the Confluent Kafka Python library.
- We will create a dictionary with the necessary configuration options as key-value pairs.
- We will instantiate the object with the configuration.
- In a for loop, we will create five records. Each record consists of the key between the number 0 to 4, and the value is the timestamp for now.

```
from confluent_kafka import Producer
import json
from datetime import datetime


conf = {'bootstrap.servers': "kafka-1:9092", 'client.id': '1'}
producer = Producer(conf)

for n in range(5):
    record_key = str(n)
    record_value = json.dumps(
                {
                    "Time": str(datetime.now())
                }
            )
    topic = "ch3_topic_1"
    producer.produce(topic, key=record_key, value=record_value)

producer.flush()
```

As we can see from the script, the record key needs to be in a string format and the message value is a JSON dictionary. The produce method[21] creates the messages asynchronously, and *producer.flush()* batch delivers the messages to the broker. On the consumer end, we will see the messages (adjusted for the timestamp, of course):

```
2,{"Time": "2021-11-02 20:08:03.389382"}
3,{"Time": "2021-11-02 20:08:03.389388"}
4,{"Time": "2021-11-02 20:08:03.389394"}
0,{"Time": "2021-11-02 20:08:03.389280"}
1,{"Time": "2021-11-02 20:08:03.389367"}
```

The messages are delivered in a batch. Thus the messages did not arrive in the order of creation on the consumer side. Remember for messages with the same key will be put in the same partition? Let's try that. If we change the key to a fixed key, such as in *ch3_producer_2.py*:

```
...
record_key = "100"
...
```

The messages will arrive in the order they were created, as shown below on the console consumer output:

```
100,{"Time": "2021-11-02 20:35:28.632326"}
100,{"Time": "2021-11-02 20:35:28.632399"}
100,{"Time": "2021-11-02 20:35:28.632411"}
100,{"Time": "2021-11-02 20:35:28.632417"}
100,{"Time": "2021-11-02 20:35:28.632423"}
```

If we want to deliver the message immediately, we can use the poll[22] method to deliver the message, as in *ch3_producer_3.py*. The returned object will contain an error code if the message encounters an error.

[21] https://docs.confluent.io/platform/current/clients/confluent-kafka-python/html/index.html#id25

[22] https://docs.confluent.io/platform/current/clients/confluent-kafka-python/html/index.html#id13

Neat, right? Let's look at the other side of the coin, consumers.

Consumers: Receiving Messages

I am a fan of the Air Jordan line of shoes[23]. It is something I developed over the years being a basketball fan. Every time they release a new or retro Air Jordan, I will anxiously wait in front of a computer and wait for the fresh pair of shoes to hit the market so I can buy them. The problem is, there are about a million other consumers who are also waiting in front of the computer, ready to click on that 'buy' button. When the shoes are released, the website site would become unresponsive and return an error.

This is a very common problem with retail and other websites that experience periodic spikes during peak times. In this case, whenever Nike releases a new model of Air Jordan shoes, the general order pipeline will be under heavy load. There can be a number of components that break under heavy load. It could be the inventory database, credit card process system, fraud protection, or a number of other components that make the response slow.

To deal with this problem, we can upgrade all the components to the level for them to handle peak volume. But there are several problems with that approach: First, it is hard to predict what peak volume is. Second, it could take a lot of time and money to upgrade all the components. Third, most of the capacity will just sit idle during normal operations.

A better way to deal with the problem is to put in a *buffer* between components and *dynamically* scale out each of the components as the situation calls for them. So, for example, we can use the Kafka

[23] https://en.wikipedia.org/wiki/Air_Jordan

cluster to queue up orders from various sources (mobile, website, store) while having multiple backend groups (inventory, credit card processing) process the orders as capacity allows.

Let's take a look at how Kafka can help in this situation, starting with consumer groups.

Consumer Groups

We can see from the producer section that multiple producers can write to a particular topic. This is not very different from other publisher-subscriber systems. What makes Kafka stand out is Kafka's ability to allow multiple consumers to read from the same topic while automatically splitting the messages between them.

The consumers in a consumer group can subscribe to a topic and choose to read the messages from the beginning or just the newer messages as they arrive. This is useful when multiple consumer groups, say inventory and credit process consumer groups, need to process messages from the same topic.

Kafka will also automatically take care of *rebalancing* the messages when new consumers are added to the consumer group or remove consumers from the consumer group when they are down. Kafka will pair up the partition to consumers in a group *at most* in a one-to-one ratio. For example, we created three partitions in ch3_topic_1. If we have one consumer in a consumer group, messages in all three partitions to be sent to that consumer. However, if we have two consumers, the messages will be load balanced between them. When we add the third consumer in that group, each partition will have a corresponding consumer. If we add a fourth consumer in the group, it will just sit idlc as a backup.

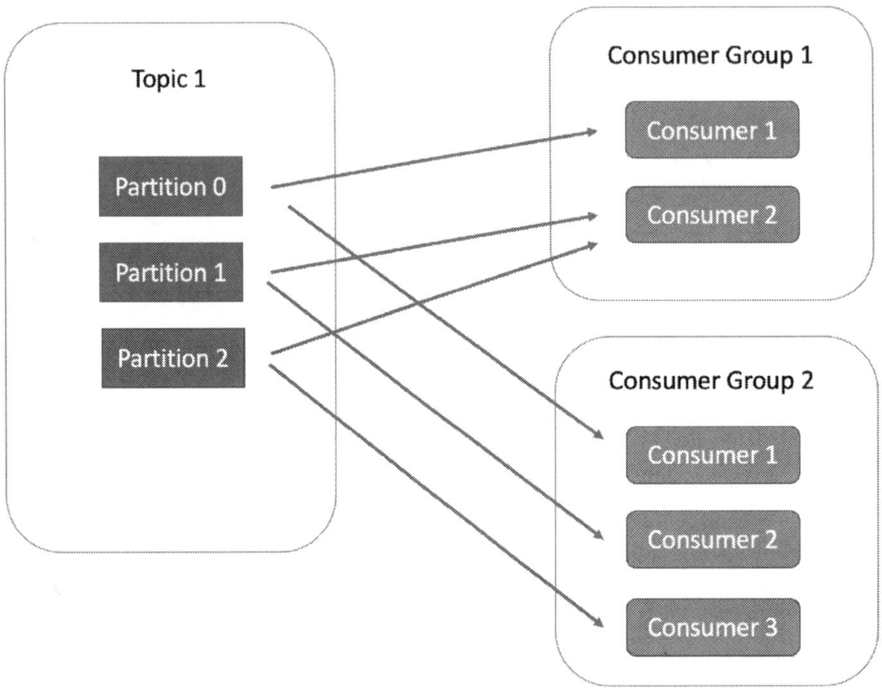

Figure 3.2 Consumer Groups

Consumer groups are one of the main features of Kafka. Typically, when we create a consumer, we will put it in a consumer group even when there is only one consumer. We can always add more consumers to the same group later.

Consumer Group Example

The first example for the consumer group will require us to open up three terminal windows, one for producer and two for consumers in the same consumer group. We will re-use the same topic we created before, *ch3_topic_1*. Let's start by using the same console consumer command we have used before with the *–group* option at the end to put them in a consumer group (do the following for the two consumer group terminals):

```
$ kafka-console-consumer.sh --bootstrap-server 127.0.0.1:9092 --topic c\
h3_topic_1 --group consumer_group_1 --property parse.key=true --propert\
y key.separator=,
```

We can start the console producer on the third terminal window:

```
$ kafka-console-producer.sh --broker-list 127.0.0.1:9092 --topic ch3_to\
pic_1 --property parse.key=true --property key.separator=,
```

We will send the following messages from the producer to Kafka:

```
>key1, I am key1 value1
>key1, I am key1 value2
>key2, I am key2 value1
>key3, I am key3 value1
>key3, I am key3 value2
>key3, I am key3 value3
```

We should start to see the messages appear on the consumer group split between the two consumers:

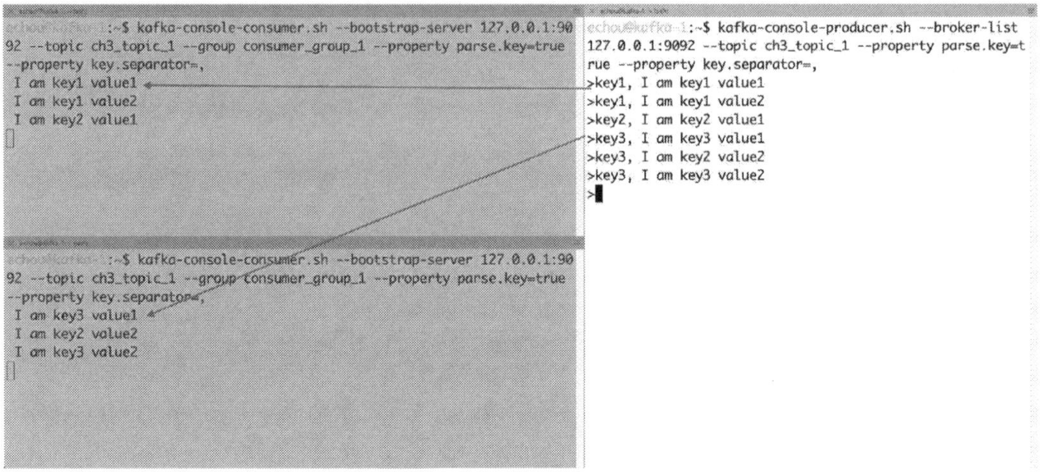

Figure 3.3 Consumer Group Messages

If we were to terminate one of the consumers, the newer messages would be sent to the remaining consumer. Thus, we can repeatedly add or remove consumers in the consumer group and Kafka will take care of the rebalancing for us.

Consumer Group with Python

As you might have imagined, consumer groups are typically set up as a long-running application that continues to poll Kafka for more data. **This polling process will also serve as a heartbeat to let Kafka know the consumer is still alive and wants to receive data**.

Below is a simple Python script, *ch3_consumer_1.py*, using the Confluent Python Kafka client[24] to produce a consumer object and poll the local Kafka cluster for records in the topic we created. This script is a simplified version of the example on the Confluent GitHub repository[25]:

[24] https://github.com/confluentinc/confluent-kafka-python

[25] https://github.com/confluentinc/examples/blob/6.2.0-post/clients/cloud/python/consumer.py

```
from confluent_kafka import Consumer


conf = {'bootstrap.servers': 'kafka-1:9092', 'group.id': 'ch3_consumer_\
group'}

consumer = Consumer(conf)
consumer.subscribe(['ch3_topic_1'])
try:
    while True:
        msg = consumer.poll(timeout=1.0)
        if msg is None:
            continue
        elif msg.error():
            print('error: {}'.format(msg.error()))
        else:
            record_key = msg.key()
            record_value = msg.value()
            print(record_key, record_value)

except KeyboardInterrupt:
    pass
finally:
    consumer.close()
```

As with the producer script, we create a Consumer object and pass in the configuration information. We can then subscribe to one or more topics in a list format. The consumer will poll the Kafka cluster every second, serving as a heartbeat for the consumer at the same time. The return message can contain an error or a success message. Before we terminate the client, it is always a good idea to close the consumer before closing. It will close the network connections and sockets. It will also trigger a rebalance immediately rather than wait for the consumer heartbeat timeout.

Please consult the Confluent Python client for Kafka documentaiton[26] for more details.

When this script launches, it will enter its while loop and listen for events. We can then use a previously built producer script, such as *ch3_producer_1.py*, to generate messages to the topic. Here is an example of the output:

```
$ python ch3_consumer_1.py
b'0' b'{"Time": "2021-11-03 15:36:31.282884"}'
b'1' b'{"Time": "2021-11-03 15:36:31.282958"}'
b'2' b'{"Time": "2021-11-03 15:36:31.282969"}'
b'3' b'{"Time": "2021-11-03 15:36:31.282975"}'
b'4' b'{"Time": "2021-11-03 15:36:31.282981"}'
```

We can also launch multiple instances of the consumer script, and Kafka will load balance the messages:

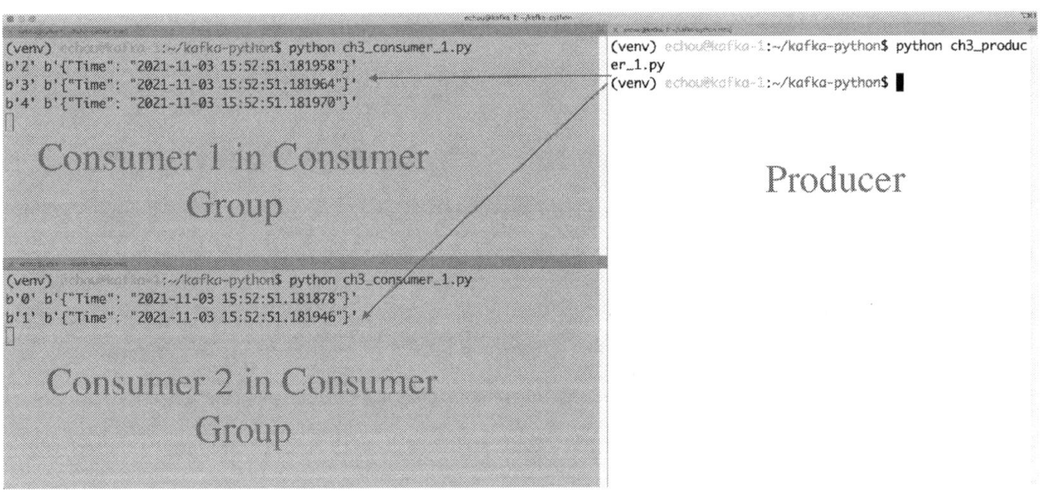

Figure 3.4 Consumer Group Load Balance Messages

For illustration, I also included a second script, *ch3_consumer_2.py*, that puts the consumer in a *different* consumer group:

[26] https://docs.confluent.io/platform/current/clients/confluent-kafka-python/html/index.html#consumer

```
...
conf = {'bootstrap.servers': 'kafka-1:9092', 'group.id': 'ch3_consumer_\
group_2'}
...
```

When launched, we can see the same message appeared to both consumers because they are in two different consumer groups:

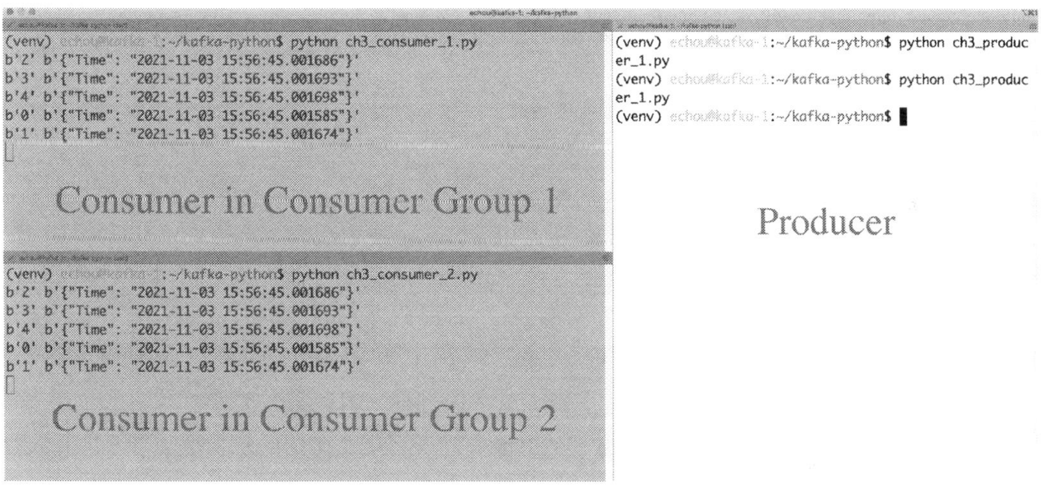

Figure 3.5 Multiple Consumer Groups

It almost seems like magic that we can scale consumers within a group. Let's look at *how* Kafka can keep track of which consumer group has received the necessary messages.

Offsets in Action

As we have learned, the *offset* number of a record in a partition indicates the position of that record. If the partition is a book, the offset is analogous to the page number of each page. When our consumer polls the message, it needs a way to update the location that it has read. Kafka calls this *commit* the offset. In our book analogy, this can be updating the bookmark of the last read page.

How does a consumer commit an offset? Kafka keeps a special topic called *__consumer_offsets* for the consumer to update the committed offset for each partition. For example, we can take a look under the *~/kafka_2.13-2.8.0/data/kafka/* directory:

```
$ ls ~/kafka_2.13-2.8.0/data/kafka/__consumer_offsets-
__consumer_offsets-0/  __consumer_offsets-18/ __consumer_offsets-27/ __\
consumer_offsets-36/ __consumer_offsets-45/
__consumer_offsets-1/  __consumer_offsets-19/ __consumer_offsets-28/ __\
consumer_offsets-37/ __consumer_offsets-46/
__consumer_offsets-10/ __consumer_offsets-2/  __consumer_offsets-29/
...
```

Clearly, the committed offset has a large implication on message processing. It is the responsibility of the consumer to indicate its latest offset. By default, the *enable.auto.commit* is set to *true*. This means when we launch our client, for every five seconds, the consumer will commit the largest offset our client has received. When we use the *close* method in the client object, we also commit the largest offset from our polls.

The *auto.commit* behavior should work in most scenarios where the clients are stable. If this is not desirable behavior, we can also use the consumer manual commit[27] provided by the consumer object.

We can use the *kafka-consumer-group* command to look at the current offset per partition. Remember the offset commits are grouped by consumer group per partition. Therefore, we need to specify the consumer group in the command:

[27] https://docs.confluent.io/platform/current/clients/confluent-kafka-python/html/index.html#confluent_kafka.Consumer.commit

```
$ kafka-consumer-groups.sh --bootstrap-server localhost:9092 --describe\
 --group ch3_consumer_group

Consumer group 'ch3_consumer_group' has no active members.

GROUP              TOPIC           PARTITION  CURRENT-OFFSET  LOG-END-O\
FFSET  LAG             CONSUMER-ID     HOST            CLIENT-ID
ch3_consumer_group ch3_topic_1     1          90              90        \
       0               -               -               -
ch3_consumer_group ch3_topic_1     2          67              67        \
       0               -               -               -
```

Let's launch the two consumers in *ch3_consumer_group* again, i.e. run *ch3_consumer_1.py* in two separate terminal windows. We should also produce some messages to the topic with *ch3_producer_1.py*. Let's look at the offsets again while they are still running:

```
$ kafka-consumer-groups.sh --bootstrap-server localhost:9092 --describe\
 --group ch3_consumer_group

GROUP              TOPIC           PARTITION  CURRENT-OFFSET  LOG-END-O\
FFSET  LAG             CONSUMER-ID                                 HOS\
T            CLIENT-ID
ch3_consumer_group ch3_topic_1     0          -               20        \
       -               rdkafka-1e4e063c-2321-438b-86b3-96441f77ccef /12\
7.0.0.1      rdkafka
ch3_consumer_group ch3_topic_1     1          102             102       \
       0               rdkafka-1e4e063c-2321-438b-86b3-96441f77ccef /12\
7.0.0.1      rdkafka
ch3_consumer_group ch3_topic_1     2          75              75        \
       0               rdkafka-ca340b10-8027-4522-9a2b-5e576e330724 /12\
7.0.0.1      rdkafka
```

Look closely and compare these outputs from the prior output, notice the statement about "active member" in the consumer group, consumer-id, and the offset numbers.

In the next section, we will take a look at administrative tasks on managing topics and partitions.

Kafka Topic Administration

The *kafka-topics.sh* tool is your best bet for most of the operations related to topics. This tool is a wrapper to call the underlying Java classes. It allows us to create, modify, delete, describe, and list our topics in the cluster. As we have seen before, we need to provide the required Zookeeper information.

We already saw how to use *kafka-topic.sh* to create a topic, for easier reference, it is listed below:

```
$ kafka-topics.sh --zookeeper 127.0.0.1:2181 --topic ch3_topic_2 --crea\
te --partitions 3 --replication-factor 1
Created topic ch3_topic_2
```

We can use the same command pattern to list the topics in the cluster:

```
$ kafka-topics.sh --zookeeper 127.0.0.1:2181 --list
...
ch3_topic_1
ch3_topic_2
...
```

To describe the topics in more detail, we can use the **-describe** switch:

```
$ kafka-topics.sh --zookeeper 127.0.0.1:2181 --describe
Topic: Test3    TopicId: EotxemaOQFG_FxGMZfnmkw PartitionCount: 1       \
 ReplicationFactor: 3    Configs: cleanup.policy=delete
        Topic: Test3    Partition: 0    Leader: 0       Replicas: 0,1,2\
 Isr: 0
Topic: __consumer_offsets       TopicId: 3PUOS-HHQhmrZvRrYZZZaQ Partiti\
onCount: 50     ReplicationFactor: 1    Configs: compression.type=prod\
ucer,cleanup.policy=compact,segment.bytes=104857600
        Topic: __consumer_offsets       Partition: 0    Leader: 0       \
 Replicas: 0     Isr: 0
        Topic: __consumer_offsets       Partition: 1    Leader: 0       \
 Replicas: 0     Isr: 0
...
```

To filter the output by a particular topic, we can append –*topic* switch at the end:

```
$ kafka-topics.sh --zookeeper 127.0.0.1:2181 --describe --topic ch3_top\
ic_2
Topic: ch3_topic_2      TopicId: lIzGyWyVQle9tSI9ojCAOw PartitionCount:\
 3       ReplicationFactor: 1    Configs:
        Topic: ch3_topic_2      Partition: 0    Leader: 0       Replica\
s: 0     Isr: 0
        Topic: ch3_topic_2      Partition: 1    Leader: 0       Replica\
s: 0     Isr: 0
        Topic: ch3_topic_2      Partition: 2    Leader: 0       Replica\
s: 0     Isr: 0
```

We can change the partition of the topic (note the warning about keys in the output below):

```
$ kafka-topics.sh --zookeeper 127.0.0.1:2181 --alter --topic ch3_topic_\
2 --partitions 6
WARNING: If partitions are increased for a topic that has a key, the pa\
rtition logic or ordering of the messages will be affected
Adding partitions succeeded!
```

If we'd like, we can delete the topics via:

```
$ kafka-topics.sh --zookeeper 127.0.0.1:2181 --delete --topic ch3_topic\
_2
Topic ch3_topic_2 is marked for deletion.
```

The *kafka-topics.sh* uses similar pattern for different operations, it is easy to get used to them with some practice. In the next section, let's talk about replication.

Replication

Replication of partitions is at the heart of high availability in Kafka. Kafka topics are broken into different partitions. Each partition can have several replicas residing on different brokers for high availability. The inner working of replication is a complex process involving leaders, in-sync replica, and replica lists. Fortunately, we do not need to worry about them to get started. We simply need to specify the number of replication during topic creation.

> For more information on Kafka partition replication, this Confluent article[28] offers a great introduction.

[28] https://www.confluent.io/blog/hands-free-kafka-replication-a-lesson-in-operational-simplicity/

So far, we have been using a replication factor of one because we only have one broker in our lab cluster. We would encounter the following error if we were to specify more than one replicator:

```
$ kafka-topics.sh --zookeeper 127.0.0.1:2181 --topic ch3_topic_2 --crea\
te --partitions 3 --replication-factor 2
WARNING: Due to limitations in metric names, topics with a period ('.')\
 or underscore ('_') could collide. To avoid issues it is best to use e\
ither, but not both.
Error while executing topic command: Replication factor: 2 larger than \
available brokers: 1.
[2021-11-03 18:16:36,928] ERROR org.apache.kafka.common.errors.InvalidR\
eplicationFactorException: Replication factor: 2 larger than available \
brokers: 1.
 (kafka.admin.TopicCommand$)
```

There are several options to solve this:

1. We can utilize public cloud providers to spin up VMs or hosted Kafka clusters quickly. We will do this in the next chapter.
2. We can launch multiple brokers in a container environment, as explained in this Confluent multi-node article[29].
3. Create multiple broker configurations and launch each as a process to simulate a multi-broker cluster as explained in this blog post[30].

For option 1, we will discuss this in detail in Chapter 4. For option 2, docker containers have their own complexities, and covering the container details is out-of-scope for this book. So we will, however, go over option 3 briefly.

There are three steps to running multiple broker processes on a single server:

[29] https://docs.confluent.io/platform/current/kafka/multi-node.html

[30] https://www.michael-noll.com/blog/2013/03/13/running-a-multi-broker-apache-kafka-cluster-on-a-single-node/

1. Copy the current servers.properties to three different files, for example, server-1.properties, server-2.properties, and server-3.properties.
2. In each of the servers.properties file, give each a unique *client.id*, unique port, and data log location. Leave everything else default.

For example:

```
# server-1.properties
broker.id=1
port=9093
log.dirs=/home/echou/kafka_2.13-2.8.0/data/kafka/kafka-logs-1

# server-2.properties
broker.id=2
port=9094
log.dirs=/home/echou/kafka_2.13-2.8.0/data/kafka/kafka-logs-2

# server-3.properties
broker.id=3
port=9095
log.dirs=/home/echou/kafka_2.13-2.8.0/data/kafka/kafka-logs-3
```

3. We can start the broker processes and reference the individual server files.

```
$ kafka-server-start.sh /home/echou/kafka-python/server-[123].properties
```

Once all three brokers registered with the Zookeeper, we now have three brokers in our cluster and can test out replication.

Conclusion

In this chapter, we went over essential concepts in Kafka. We begin with producing messages using both the CLI tool as well as Python library. After the producer example, we saw how we could use consumer groups to load balance messages between multiple consumers. We also used the CLI tool to perform various administrative tasks for topics. Toward the end of the chapter, we looked at simulating multiple brokers on a single host.

In the next chapter, we will look at how to launch hosted Kafka cluster on Amazon AWS.

Chapter 4. Hosted Kafka Services

In the last chapter, we looked at the operations for producers and consumers and applied the concepts we have learned along the way. The producer was used to construct a message, serialize data, determine the partition, then transport it to Kafka Broker. We used consumer groups to allow multiple consumers to subscribe to the same topic. Kafka will dynamically split the messages between the consumers and rebalance the messages when consumers leave or join the groups.

The commits and offsets allow Kafka to keep track of the necessary progress of processed messages by topic and consumer groups. The best part about most of the examples we saw, in my opinion, is that Kafka handles all of the complexities automatically for us. Of course, we should understand the concepts in case we need to troubleshoot for any issues, but for the most part, the operations should work automatically for us.

Now that we have some familiarity with Kafka operations in a lab setup, you might be wondering how we can move this into a production environment. Similar to many at-scale services nowadays, there is an ecosystem of Kafka-as-a-Service ready to be used by us. If you are like most people, managing Kafka cluster is most likely not the core competency of your business or role. If we can offload the management overhead to somebody else, we can spend our time and energy on the business and data flow. In my opinion, as a first step outside of the lab, we can, and should, take advantage of the managed Kafka services.

There are generally two types of managed Kafka services, which can be a source of confusion for some. There is a Kafka cluster hosting option. We can specify the configuration of our cluster, and the hosting company will launch the cluster for us. Companies offer this hosting option, such as Amazon with Amazon Managed Stream for Apache Kafka (Amazon MSK)[31] and Confluent with Confluent Cloud[32].

The second managed service option is to utilize the service by just the message topic. In this case, we do not have visibility to the cluster. Instead, we simply get an endpoint or SDK to point our producers and consumers to. This type of service is generally an adaption of Kafka by the cloud providers. So, these services have various degrees of Kafka compatibility.

In this chapter, we will look at the cluster hosting offering by Amazon MSK. The next chapter will look at the topic hosting options using Amazon Kinesis, Azure Event Hub, and Google Cloud Pub/Sub.

> The reason for picking Amazon MSK over Confluent Cloud is because AWS has a complete product portfolio. As we know, Kafka is a middleware that integrates with other services. By using Amazon MSK, we can better integrate Kafka with AWS services, such as identity management, Serverless Lambda functions, and other services.

Let us begin with an overview of Amazon Managed Streaming for Apache Kafka.

[31] https://aws.amazon.com/msk/
[32] https://www.confluent.io/confluent-cloud/

AWS Managed Kafka Service

Amazon Managed Streaming for Apache Kafka (MSK) was launched on May 30th, 2019. The service was made generally available in September of 2021. The overall premise of the service is pretty simple and straightforward, we use the AWS CLI or portal to create the cluster, specify the number and type of EC2 instance our Brokers and Zookeepers will live in, and Amazon MSK will take care of the rest:

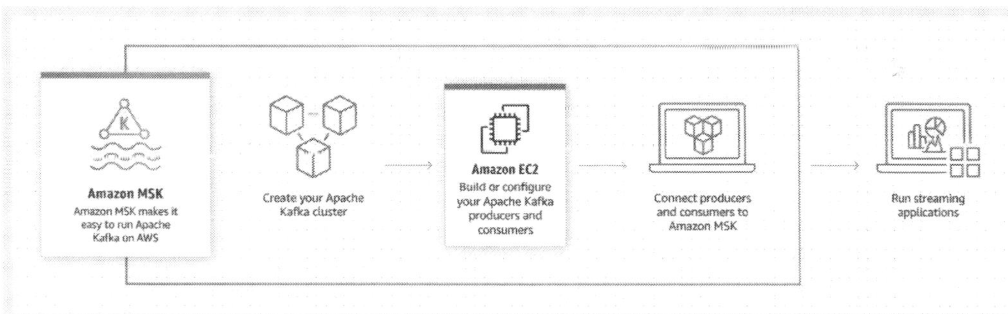

Amazon MSK Overview (source: https://aws.amazon.com/msk/)

After the cluster is provisioned, we will receive connection strings. The connection string is how we can connect to the Kafka cluster.

> Amazon MSK is a relatively new service, and it might not be available in the region of your choice. However, at the time of writing, it is available in 17 AWS regions, check the AWS Regional Services List[33] for the latest services available by region.

As we could imagine, the Amazon MSK service can be integrated with other AWS services such as IAM, Amazon Virtual Private Cloud, AWS

[33] https://aws.amazon.com/about-aws/global-infrastructure/regional-product-services/

Certificate Manager, Private Certificate Authorities, and AWS Key Management Service. Running the Kafka cluster within AWS cloud has the additional benefits 99.9 availability Service-Level-Agreement. Since we do not manage the Zookeeper or Kafka brokers directly, this significantly reduced the management overhead. We also have cluster-wide storage scaling. However, AWS forces even storage scaling amongst the brokers, so we need to have identical storage space between all of our Kafka brokers.

In summary, the benefits of having AWS MSK are:

- Apache Kafka compatible: This is the fully open-source version of Kafka. The applications, tooling, and plugins developed by the Apache Kafka ecosystem are supported and compatible.
- Fully managed: As we have stressed, we do not need to worry about the provisioning, configuration, and maintenance of the Kafka cluster. The reduced operational overhead would allow us to focus on our application features and data management.
- Highly available: AWS maintains highly available regions and zones around the globe.

At the time of writing, Amazon MSK supports Apache Kafka 2.1.0. Let's take a look at how much the service cost.

Amazon MSK Costs

As with most Amazon AWS services, MSK is a region-based service. This means the resource prices are dependent on the region we run our services in. The services are built upon Amazon EC2 virtual machines with basic fees. The EC2 instance will need to be t3.small or above, which means we cannot use smaller instances such as t3.nano or t3.micro.

The main categories of charges we need to be concerned with are:

- The time the broker instances run.
- The storage we use monthly.
- The data transfer in and out of the cluster.

We do not need to pay for Apache Zookeeper nodes that Amazon MSK provisioned for us. Please use the MSK pricing page[34] to check on the latest pricing. We can also use the MSK price calculator[35] to estimate the monthly cost.

> As a reference, for writing this chapter, I ran the small *Kafka.t3.small* cluster for a few hours in *US East (N. Virginia)* for less than USD $5.

If you are not sure which region to choose, at the time of writing, *US East (N. Virginia)* and *US West (Oregon)* have the lowest per hour pricing. These two regions are good options for running a small production cluster. As a reference, for *kafka.t3.small* instances in *US East (N. Virginia)*, they are billed at *USD $0.0456* per hour. Depending on our traffic pattern, if we only need the cluster to run at certain hours, we can launch the cluster only when we need them. This would keep the cost manageable.

---

[34] https://aws.amazon.com/msk/pricing/

[35] https://calculator.aws/#/createCalculator/MSK

Broker Instance Pricing Tables

Region: US West (Oregon)

Broker Instance	Price Per Hour
kafka.t3.small - vCPU: 2, Memory (GiB): 2	$0.0456
kafka.m5.large - vCPU: 2, Memory (GiB): 8	$0.21
kafka.m5.xlarge - vCPU: 4, Memory (GiB): 16	$0.42
kafka.m5.2xlarge - vCPU: 8, Memory (GiB): 32	$0.84
kafka.m5.4xlarge - vCPU: 16, Memory (GiB): 64	$1.68
kafka.m5.8xlarge - vCPU: 32, Memory (GiB): 128	$3.36
kafka.m5.12xlarge - vCPU: 48, Memory (GiB): 192	$5.04
kafka.m5.16xlarge - vCPU: 64, Memory (GiB): 256	$6.73
kafka.m5.24xlarge - vCPU: 96, Memory (GiB): 394	$10.08

Figure 4.2 Broker Instance Pricing Tables

> Again, we are billed by the usage. Please remember to shut down the cluster when we are done to avoid unnecessary charges.

For the most part, Amazon MKS is compatible with the open-source Apache Kafka project. However, there are some differences between them, such as the type of Schema Registry that can be used by producers. For more detailed commonly asked questions, please take a look at the Amazon MSK Q&A page[36].

Let's go ahead and launch our first cluster.

Launch Amazon MSK Cluster

To launch an Amazon MSK Cluster, here are the general steps:

1. Create a VPC if you do not already have one.

[36] https://aws.amazon.com/msk/faqs/

2. Create High Availability subnets if it is a new VPC.
3. Create an MSK Cluster.
4. Create a Client machine within the VPC if this is a new VPC.

We will start by creating a VPC.

Creating VPC

Amazon MSK needs to be launched within Amazon Virtual Private Cloud (VPC). If you are not familiar with VPC, it can be thought of as a private network or subnet within the AWS cloud. Feel free to use an existing VPC if you already have one. If you do not have one or prefer to create a new one, this section provides a step-by-step guide. At the time of writing, the default VPC limit is five per region.

I am going to create a VPC in US-East-1 with a single public subnet:

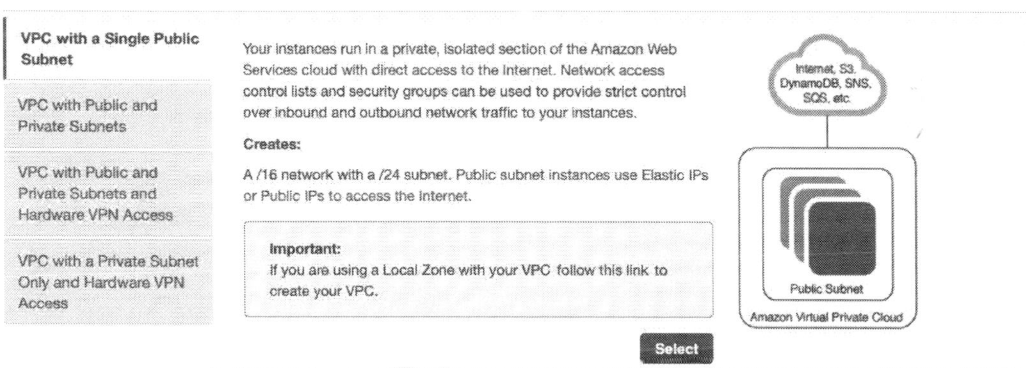

Figure 4.3 VPC with a Single Public Subnet

Here are the VPC parameters:

- VPC Name: MSKTestingVPC
- Public subnet's IPv4 CIDR: 10.0.1.0/24

- Availability Zone: us-east-1a
- Subnet name: MSKTestingSubnet-1

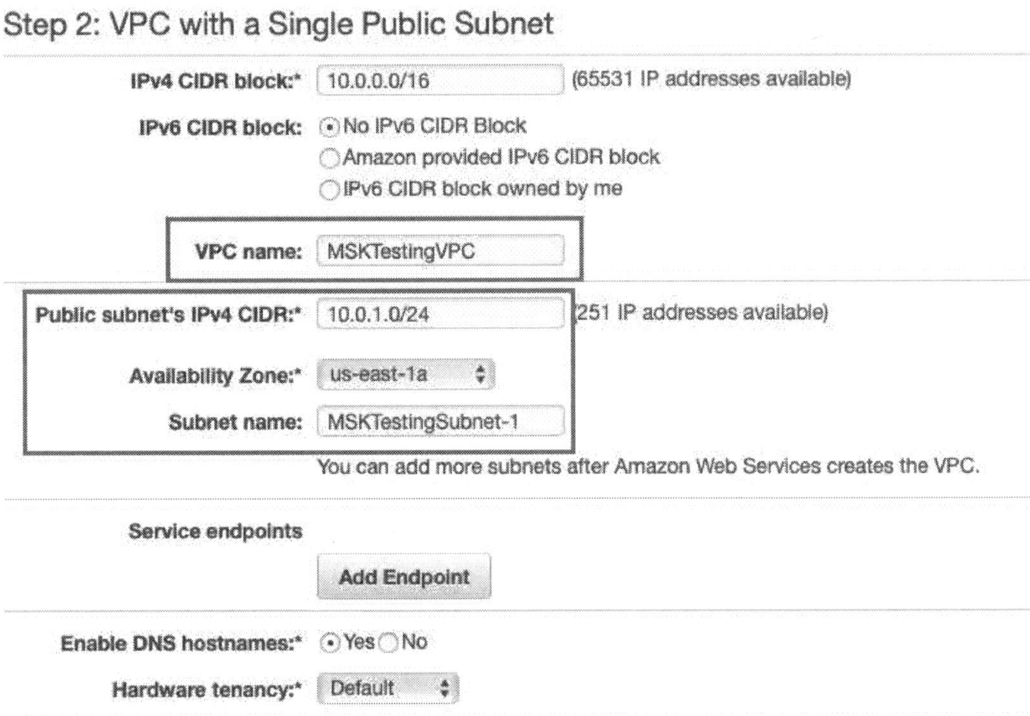

Figure 4.4 VPC parameters

Once the VPC is created, take a note of the VPC ID. The VPC ID is a set of words started with *vpc-<number>*. We will need to use it in later steps. We will also need to go into the subnet menu for our newly created subnet, and write down the route table associated with that subnet. The route table ID is a set of words started with *rtb-<number>*. Again, we will need this id in later steps.

Create High Availability subnets

Each AWS region has several availability zones. The availability zones are geographically dispersed data centers within the region. We will create two additional subnets in different availability zones. This setup allows us for better assurance of not having multiple brokers going down from a single region failure.

For the us-east-1 region, we can use us-east-1b and us-east-1c availability zones for the additional subnets. We will create the second subnets with the following parameters:

- Pick the existing *MSKTestingVPC* from list
- Subnet name: MSKTEstingSubnet-2
- Availability Zone: us-east-1b
- IPv4 CIDR: 10.0.2.0/24

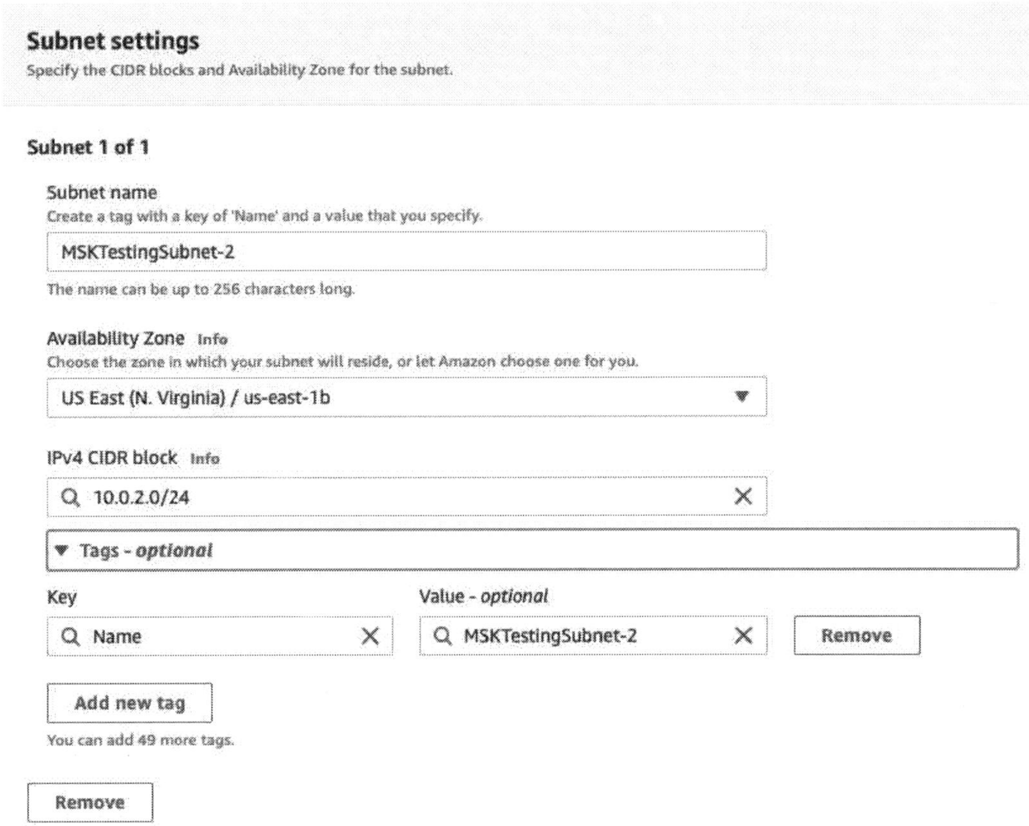

Figure 4.5 VPC subnet 2

The third subnet parameters are as follows:

- Pick the existing *MSKTestingVPC* from list
- Subnet name: MSKTEstingSubnet-3
- Availability Zone: us-east-1c
- IPv4 CIDR: 10.0.3.0/24

Once the two additional subnets are created, we will associate the two subnets with the previous routing table. We will do this by clicking on the check box next to the newly created subnets, pick the route table tab, then click on *Edit route table association*:

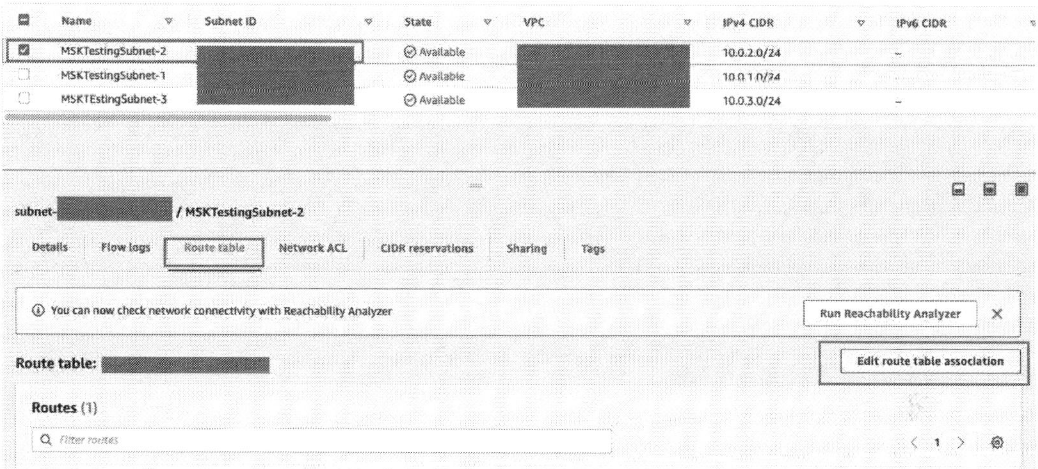

Figure 4.6 Change Route Table

Once that is done, we are ready to create the Amazon MSK Cluster.

Create an MSK Cluster.

To create a cluster, we will use the *AWS console -> Amazon MSK -> Create Cluster.* We can choose the *custom create* option:

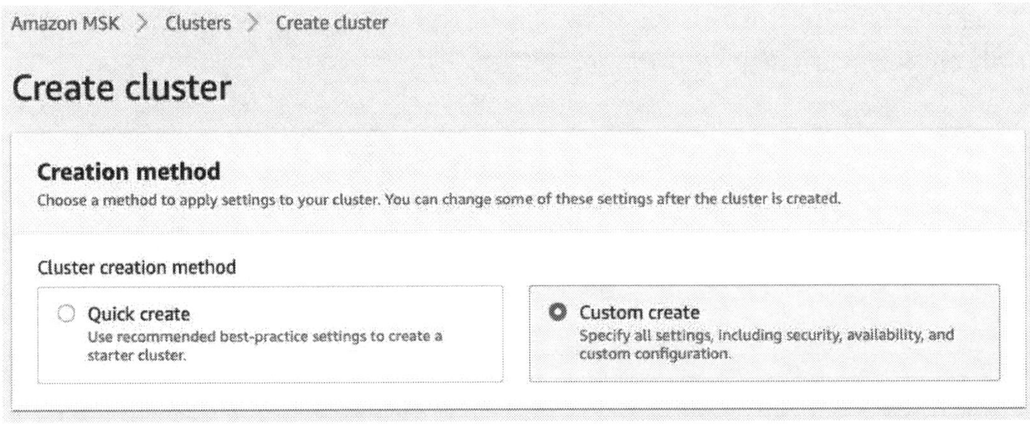

Figure 4.7 Create MSK Cluster

We will use the following parameters:

- Cluster name: MKSTesting-cluster-1
- Apache Kafka version: 2.6.2
- Under networking, choose the VPC we created in the last step.
- For the number of zones, pick 3.
- Choose us-east-1a for the first zone, pick MSKTestingSubnet-1 from the drop-down menu.
- Repeat last step for us-east-1b and us-east-1c.
- Broker Type: kafka.t3.small
- EBS storage volume per broker: 50GB

We can leave the rest of the options as default. Creating a new Kafka cluster will take a while, it may take up to 15 minutes for the creation. Once the cluster is created, we need a client to communicate with it. We will create a new Kafka client in the next step.

Create a Client machine

Currently, the MSK cluster can only be accessed from within the VPC. This means the Kafka clients will need access to the VPC. This can be done with a client residing in the VPC or with private connections via VPN or ExpressRoute. There is no direct public internet option for client access, as explained in the Amazon MSK FAQ[37]:

> **Q: Is it possible to connect to my cluster over the public Internet?**
> Amazon MSK does not support public endpoints. It is however possible to use virtual private network (VPN) connectivity between your clients and your Amazon VPC to connect to your Amazon MSK cluster.

For us, we will launch an EC2 client inside of the VPC to access the cluster. For this instance, I will pick a virtual machine with the following parameters:

- Amazon Machine Image: Ubuntu Server 20.04 LTS
- Instance type: t2.small
- Pick the VPC we created.
- Pick the subnets from us-east-1a.
- We will assign a public IP to the instance so we can ssh to it.

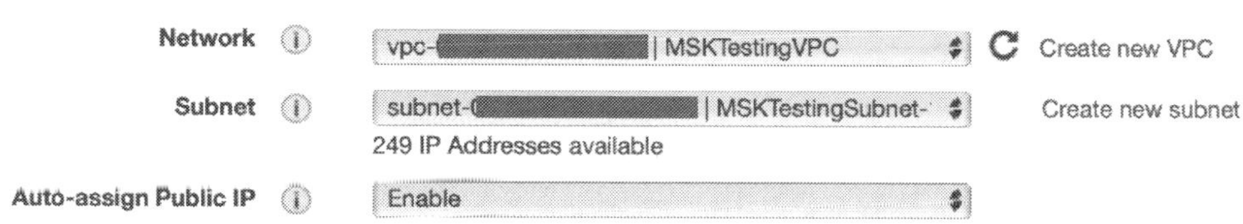

Figure 4.8 EC2 Instance Network Details

- We can choose to use an existing key pair or generate new pair for SSH access.

[37] https://aws.amazon.com/msk/faqs/

Once the client is launched, copy the security group ID for the client. It is the set of words that starts with *sgr-<number>*. We will need to allow this group inbound access to the VPC of the Kafka cluster.

Here are the steps to allow the security group access to the Kafka VPC:

- From the VPC dashboard, pick Security Groups.
- Under the column of VPC ID, find the ID that corresponds to the VPC ID we created.
- Check the box next to that security group
- On the bottom management menu, click on inbound rules, then click on *Edit inbound rules.*
- We will allow *all traffic* sourced from a custom source. The source will be the security group of our client.

Figure 4.9 VPC Security Group Inbound

This is probably the most tricky part of the steps, but as long as we match up the VPC ID and the security group ID, we are ok.

Client Setup

On the new client, first we will install the AWS CLI tool so we can query the cluster:

```
$ sudo apt update && sudo apt upgrade
$ sudo apt install awscli
```

Once the tool is installed, we will configure the AWS CLI with the necessary credentials. The credentials are an access key and secret access key pair associated with a user. The user needs to be an administrator or someone with access to the AWS MSK service.

If you are not familiar with access keys for IAM users, please take a look at this IAM User Guide[38]. We will use the *aws configure* command to enter the access credentials:

```
$ aws configure
AWS Access Key ID [None]: <your key>
AWS Secret Access Key [None]: <your secret key>
Default region name [None]: us-east-1
Default output format [None]: json
```

All of AWS resources are identified with an ARN (AWS Resource Number) number. We can find the ARN for our MSK Cluster on the cluster page:

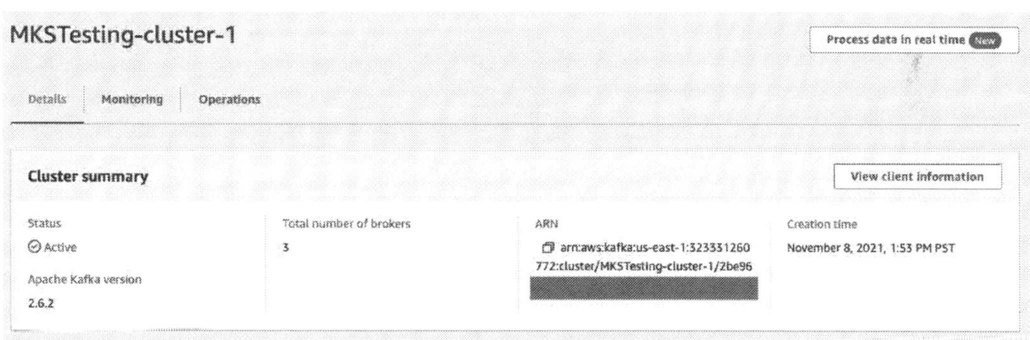

Figure 4.10 MSK ARN ID

To find the connection string for our cluster, we will use AWS CLI to query the cluster for the cluster information:

[38] https://docs.aws.amazon.com/IAM/latest/UserGuide/id_credentials_access-keys.html

```
$ aws kafka describe-cluster --region us-east-1 --cluster-arn "arn:aws:\
kafka:us-east-1:<skip>:cluster/MKSTesting-cluster-1/<skip>"
```

We will see a lot of information regarding the cluster:


```
{
    "ClusterInfo": {
        "BrokerNodeGroupInfo": {
            "BrokerAZDistribution": "DEFAULT",
            "ClientSubnets": [
                "subnet-",
                "subnet-",
                "subnet-"
            ],
            "InstanceType": "kafka.t3.small",
            "SecurityGroups": [
                "sg-"
            ],
            "StorageInfo": {
                "EbsStorageInfo": {
                    "VolumeSize": 50
                }
            }
        },
        "ClientAuthentication": {
            "Tls": {
                "CertificateAuthorityArnList": []
            }
        },
        "ClusterArn": "arn:aws:kafka:us-east-1::cluster/MKSTesting-clus\
ter-1/",
        "ClusterName": "MKSTesting-cluster-1",
        "CreationTime": "2021-11-08T21:53:33.273Z",
        "CurrentBrokerSoftwareInfo": {
            "KafkaVersion": "2.6.2"
```

```
        },
        "CurrentVersion": "",
        "EncryptionInfo": {
            "EncryptionAtRest": {
                "DataVolumeKMSKeyId": "arn:aws:kms:us-east-1::key/"
            },
            "EncryptionInTransit": {
                "ClientBroker": "TLS_PLAINTEXT",
                "InCluster": true
            }
        },
        "EnhancedMonitoring": "DEFAULT",
        "OpenMonitoring": {
            "Prometheus": {
                "JmxExporter": {
                    "EnabledInBroker": false
                },
                "NodeExporter": {
                    "EnabledInBroker": false
                }
            }
        },
        "LoggingInfo": {
            "BrokerLogs": {
                "CloudWatchLogs": {
                    "Enabled": false
                },
                "Firehose": {
                    "Enabled": false
                },
                "S3": {
                    "Enabled": false
                }
            }
        },
        "NumberOfBrokerNodes": 3,
```

```
            "State": "ACTIVE",
            "Tags": {},
            "ZookeeperConnectString": "z-3.mkstesting-cluster-1.s7my8w.c19.\
kafka.us-east-1.amazonaws.com:2181,z-1.mkstesting-cluster-1.s7my8w.c19.\
kafka.us-east-1.amazonaws.com:2181,z-2.mkstesting-cluster-1.s7my8w.c19.\
kafka.us-east-1.amazonaws.com:2181"
        }
}
```

What we are are primarily interested in is the Zookeeper connection string at the bottom of the output. Once we have that, we can create the topic via console tools. Let's go ahead and repeat what we did to install Kafka console tools:

```
$ sudo apt install openjdk-8-jdk
$ curl -O https://archive.apache.org/dist/kafka/2.8.0/kafka_2.13-2.8.0.\
tgz
$ tar -xvzf kafka_2.13-2.8.0.tgz
$ vim ~/.bashrc
...
export PATH=/home/ubuntu/kafka_2.13-2.8.0/bin:$PATH
...
```

Now, let's create a topic, *ch4_topic_1*, in our new Amazon MKS Cluster with the Zookeeper connection string:

```
$ kafka-topics.sh --create --zookeeper z-3.mkstesting-cluster-1.s7my8w.\
c19.kafka.us-east-1.amazonaws.com:2181,z-1.mkstesting-cluster-1.s7my8w.\
c19.kafka.us-east-1.amazonaws.com:2181,z-2.mkstesting-cluster-1.s7my8w.\
c19.kafka.us-east-1.amazonaws.com:2181 --replication-factor 3 --partiti\
ons 3 --topic ch4_topic_1

Created topic ch4_topic_1.
```

Fantastic! Notice the replication factor is three for this cluster. We now have a hosted Kafka cluster with geographic redundancy. It is living in the Amazon cloud. We are on a roll, let's produce and consume some data.

Produce and Consume Data

We know where the Zookeepers are, but where are the Kafka brokers? Of course, before we can produce messages, we would need to get the Kafka brokers' information. We can query the broker information with the *get-bootstrap-brokers* option:

```
$ aws kafka get-bootstrap-brokers --region us-east-1 --cluster-arn "arn\
:aws:kafka:us-east-1:323331260772:cluster/MKSTesting-cluster-1/2be96c81\
-22aa-4a00-881f-7ccecdeaf735-19"
{
    "BootstrapBrokerString": "b-1.mkstesting-cluster-1.s7my8w.c19.kafka\
.us-east-1.amazonaws.com:9092,b-2.mkstesting-cluster-1.s7my8w.c19.kafka\
.us-east-1.amazonaws.com:9092,b-3.mkstesting-cluster-1.s7my8w.c19.kafka\
.us-east-1.amazonaws.com:9092",
    "BootstrapBrokerStringTls": "b-1.mkstesting-cluster-1.s7my8w.c19.ka\
fka.us-east-1.amazonaws.com:9094,b-2.mkstesting-cluster-1.s7my8w.c19.ka\
fka.us-east-1.amazonaws.com:9094,b-3.mkstesting-cluster-1.s7my8w.c19.ka\
fka.us-east-1.amazonaws.com:9094"
}
```

We have two connections strings. We will use the plain *BootstrapBrokerString*, not the TLS string. Now we can use the console producer to produce data to the topic *ch4_topic_1*:

```
$ kafka-console-producer.sh --broker-list b-1.mkstesting-cluster-1.s7my\
8w.c19.kafka.us-east-1.amazonaws.com:9092,b-2.mkstesting-cluster-1.s7my\
8w.c19.kafka.us-east-1.amazonaws.com:9092,b-3.mkstesting-cluster-1.s7my\
8w.c19.kafka.us-east-1.amazonaws.com:9092 --topic ch4_topic_1
```

We can use the console consumer to receive the data from this topic:

```
$ kafka-console-consumer.sh --bootstrap-server b-1.mkstesting-cluster-1\
.s7my8w.c19.kafka.us-east-1.amazonaws.com:9092,b-2.mkstesting-cluster-1\
.s7my8w.c19.kafka.us-east-1.amazonaws.com:9092,b-3.mkstesting-cluster-1\
.s7my8w.c19.kafka.us-east-1.amazonaws.com:9092 --topic ch4_topic_1
```

Here is a screenshot of the side-by-side messages for producer and consumer:

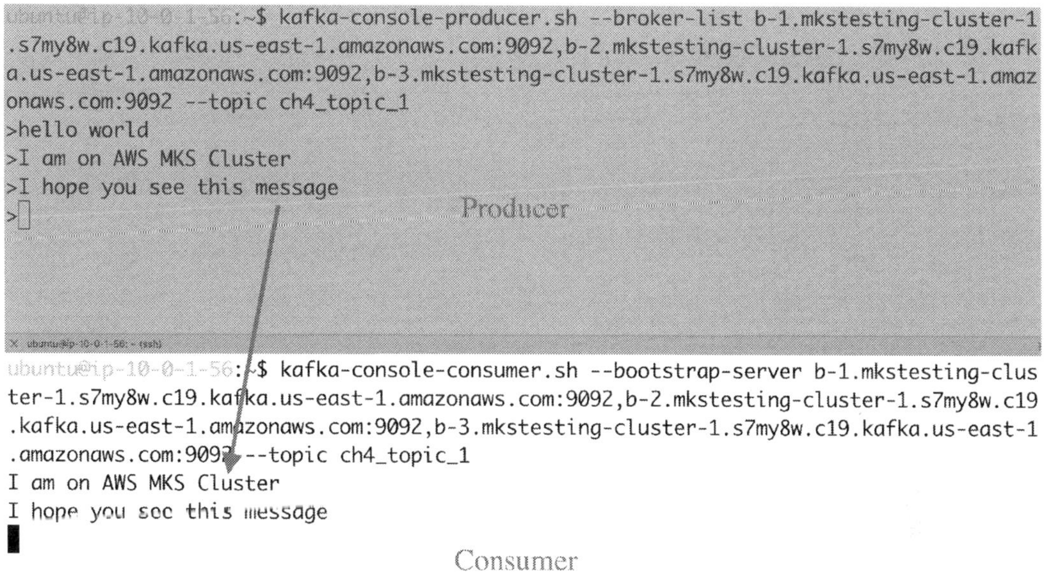

Figure 4.11 MSK Producer and Consumer

How cool is that? Within only a few minutes, we can launch a whole Kafka cluster without dealing with most of the management overhead. We can launch this cluster when we need and shut it down when we don't.

Since the cluster is hosted in AWS, we can leverage existing CloudWatch monitoring to monitor our cluster. The graph below was obtained from *CloudWatch -> Metrics -> All metrics -> AWS/Kafka Broker ID, Cluster Name*:

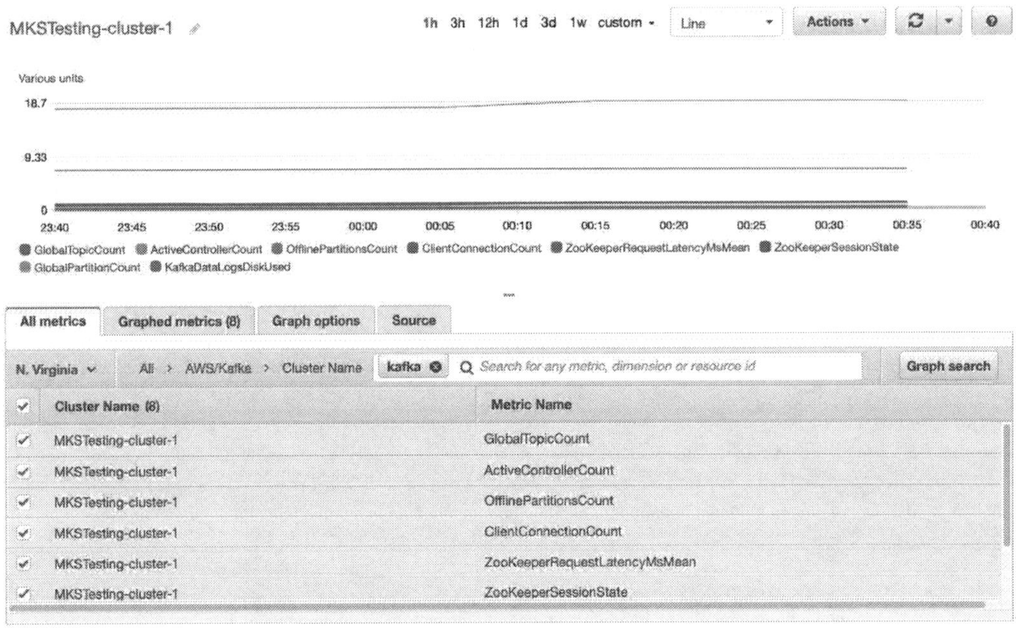

Figure 4.12 CloudWatch Monitoring

Once we are done with the example, we can delete it to avoid additional usage charges.

Conclusion

We live in an amazing time of utility computing. With the public cloud providers, we can utilize computing resources with a few clicks of the finger. When we are ready to launch a Kafka cluster in production, we can use a hosted option for our Kafka cluster. In this chapter, we saw the steps of how we can do that.

In the next chapter, we will take a tour of an alternative of using hosted Kafka cluster. We will see how we can use the public cloud provider's adapted version of messaging services, namely AWS Kinesis, Azure

Event Hub, and Google Cloud Pub/Sub.

Chapter 5. Cloud Provider Messaging Services

Chapter 4 saw how we could use hosted Kafka service to launch a production-ready Kafka cluster. Compared to building our colocation or an on-premise server, hosted Kafka service is a much quicker and arguably lower cost option. However, it does seem like a big jump to move from a single server lab device to a multi-server, always-on production environment. In addition, the cost associated with running a production cluster seems high if we only needed one or two topics with a few producers-subscribers combination.

One way we can scale slowly from lab to a full Kafka cluster, hosted or not, is to use managed event streaming services from the cloud providers. If you are familiar with the *everything-as-a-service* offerings, such as Office 365 or AWS Lambda, a managed event streaming service is very similar to them. We basically create a topic, receive an endpoint from the cloud provider, and start publishing and subscribing to them. This is especially useful if our service is already residing at one of the cloud providers that offer this service. We can take advantage of the existing setup such as identity management, cost center, console tools, and other services along with the new data streaming capabilities.

There is good and bad news with this approach. The good news is most major cloud providers (Amazon AWS, Microsoft Azure, Google Cloud) all offer data streaming services. The bad news is they have various degrees of Kafka compatibility. The compatibility scale can range from zero mentioning in Amazon Kinesis to full Kafka compatibility in Azure

Event Hubs for Apache Kafka[39]. As with many things in life, the choice of picking a messaging service versus full Kafka cluster is a trade-off between speed and future-proofing. Therefore, we should learn about the various options and make the call based on the available information to us.

In this chapter, we will take a look at the data streaming offerings from the top three public cloud providers by market share:

- Amazon Kinesis[40]
- Azure Event Hub[41]
- GCP Pub/Sub[42]

Let's start with Amazon Kinesis.

Amazon Kinesis

We saw Amazon MSK in the last chapter, compare to Amazon MSK, Amazon Kinesis is older and more mature. According to the Kinesis product page[43], Kinesis is a service that 'easily collects, processes, and analyze video and data streams in real-time'.

There are three types of streams we can create:

- Kinesis Data Streams
- Kinesis Data Firehose
- Kinesis Data Analytics.

[39]https://azure.microsoft.com/en-us/blog/announcing-the-general-availability-of-azure-event-hubs-for-apache-kafka/
[40]https://aws.amazon.com/kinesis/
[41]https://azure.microsoft.com/en-us/services/event-hubs/#overview
[42]https://cloud.google.com/pubsub/
[43]https://aws.amazon.com/kinesis/

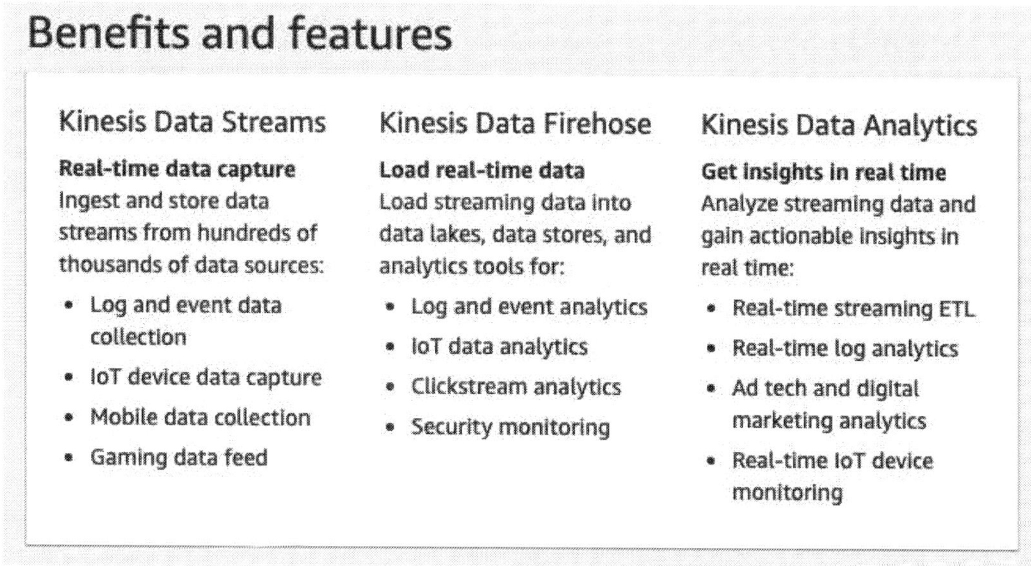

Figure 5.1 AWS Kinesis Streams

Kinesis Data Firehose is mainly used for a service-to-service stream with sources such as CloudWatch VPC Flowlogs. They provide an easy way to pick an existing AWS data source to be streamed to the messaging bus.

On the other hand, Kinesis Data Analytics is used for getting insights from AWS' analytics services. They are mainly used with the Amazon Kinesis Data Analytics service to automatically query and analyze streaming data. The results can be sent to another AWS service, such as Amazon S3 or another Amazon Kinesis Data Streams.

Kinesis Data Streams is the original data streams feed with fewer guard rails. Therefore, we will use the Kinesis Data Stream for the example in the next section.

Amazon Kinesis Example

There are two parts to working with Amazon Kinesis. The first part is a general setup for AWS command-line tools (CLI). This is a one-time setup process. If you already have AWS CLI installed and set up on your machine, please feel free to skip step 1 below.

Please remember to activate the Python virtual environment.

The second part of the example is specific to Amazon Kinesis. We will use the Boto3 library to create a topic, produce messages, and receive the messages by subscribing to the topic.

1. Install AWS CLI and populate credentials from an IAM user with access to Kinesis:

```
$ sudo apt install awscli
$ aws configure
AWS Access Key ID [None]: <insert your own access key>
AWS Secret Access Key [None]: <insert you own secret access key>
Default region name [None]: <opitonal>
Default output format [None]: <optional>
```

2. Install Boto3 Python library:

```
$ pip install boto3
```

3. Create AWS Kinesis data stream named *kinesis-test-stream* via the AWS portal:

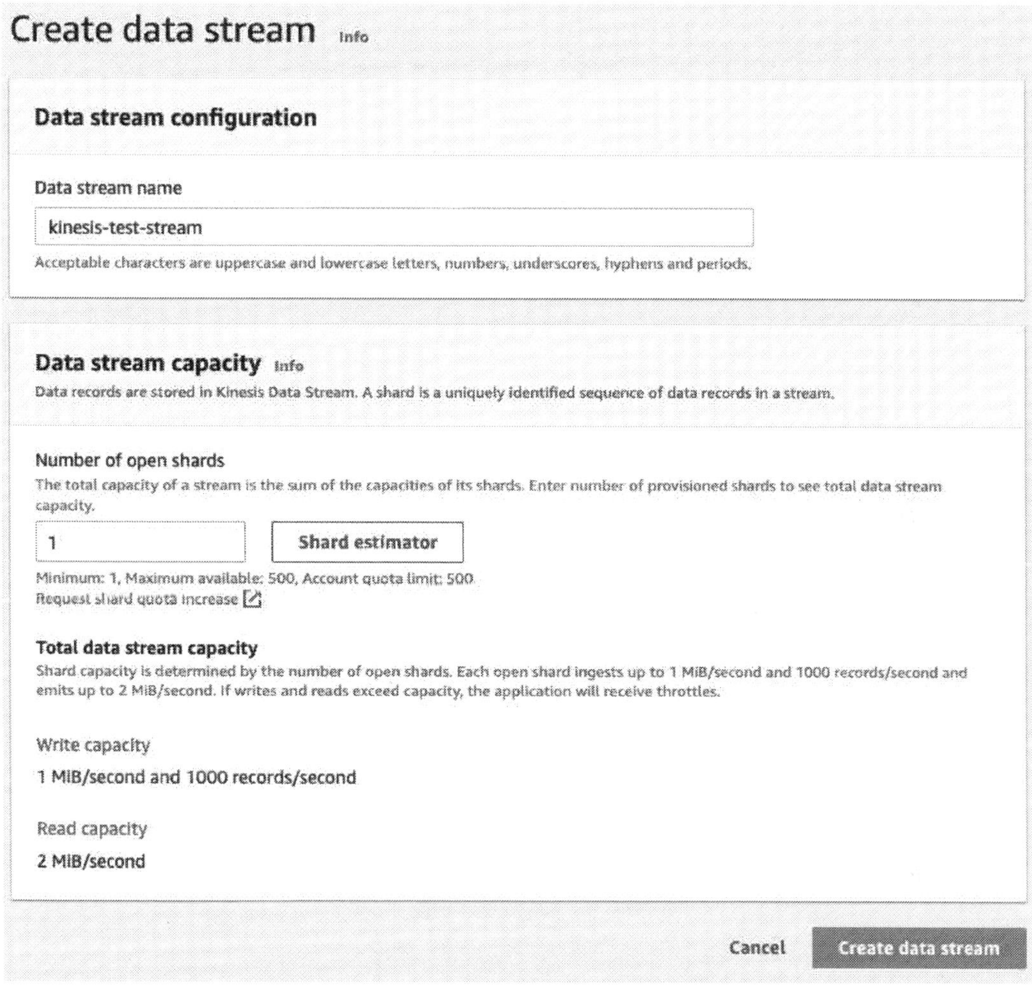

Figure 5.2 AWS Create Data Stream

4. Create a Python producer script, *ch5 gcp_publisher.py*. The script is an example modified from the Getting Started with Kinesis Python blog post[44].

[44] https://www.arundhaj.com/blog/getting-started-kinesis-python.html

```python
# Example from https://www.arundhaj.com/blog/getting-started-kinesis-py\
thon.html
import boto3
import json
from datetime import datetime
import calendar
import random
import time

my_stream_name = 'kinesis-test-stream'

kinesis_client = boto3.client('kinesis', region_name='us-west-2')

def put_to_stream(thing_id, property_value, property_timestamp):
    payload = {
                'prop': str(property_value),
                'timestamp': str(property_timestamp),
                'thing_id': thing_id
              }

    print(payload)

    put_response = kinesis_client.put_record(
                        StreamName=my_stream_name,
                        Data=json.dumps(payload),
                        PartitionKey=thing_id)

while True:
    property_value = random.randint(40, 120)
    property_timestamp = calendar.timegm(datetime.utcnow().timetuple())
    thing_id = 'aa-bb'

    put_to_stream(thing_id, property_value, property_timestamp)

    # wait for 5 second
    time.sleep(5)
```

As we can see from the script, we use the Boto3 Python library to handle most of the client work. The most crucial piece of information from the producer code would be the *partition key*. A partition key is used to segregate and route records to different shards of a data stream. This is analogous to the message key in Kafka. Having the same partition key ensures the data records will arrive at the data stream in the order they are received.

> A *shard* is the base throughput unit of an Amazon Kinesis data stream. One shard provides a capacity of 1MB/sec data input and 2MB/sec data output.

Two of the valuable resources for working with Kinesis Data Streams are:

- Kinesis Data Streams FAQ[45]
- Boto3 Kinesis Client[46]

Once the producer is ready, we can create a consumer.

5. Create a Python consumer script, *ch5_aws_subscriber.py*, as a subscriber:

[45] https://aws.amazon.com/kinesis/data-streams/faqs/

[46] https://boto3.amazonaws.com/v1/documentation/api/latest/reference/services/kinesis.html

```
# Example from https://www.arundhaj.com/blog/getting-started-kinesis-py\
thon.html
import boto3
import json
from datetime import datetime
import time

my_stream_name = 'kinesis-test-stream'

kinesis_client = boto3.client('kinesis', region_name='us-west-2')

response = kinesis_client.describe_stream(StreamName=my_stream_name)

my_shard_id = response['StreamDescription']['Shards'][0]['ShardId']

shard_iterator = kinesis_client.get_shard_iterator(StreamName=my_stream\
_name,
                                                      ShardId=my_shard_\
id,
                                                      ShardIteratorType\
='LATEST')

my_shard_iterator = shard_iterator['ShardIterator']

record_response = kinesis_client.get_records(ShardIterator=my_shard_ite\
rator,
                                              Limit=2)

while 'NextShardIterator' in record_response:
    record_response = kinesis_client.get_records(ShardIterator=record_r\
esponse['NextShardIterator'], Limit=2)

    print(record_response)

    # wait for 5 seconds
    time.sleep(5)
```

As we can see, the subscriber script uses the same kinesis client from Boto3 Python library. The crucial information from the subscriber is the usage of the *shard_iterator*. A shard iterator specifies the shard position from which to start reading the data records. How does Kinesis Stream specify the location of the records? The location is specified via a *sequence number*. Every record in the stream is identified by a sequence number when the record is put into the stream. The sequence number is analogous to Kafka offset.

After we specified the shard iterator, we configured the number of records to receive and how often we wanted to receive the records. Let's launch the subscriber script.

6. We will launch the subscriber script and let it run:

```
$ python ch5_aws_subscriber.py
```

7. We will use the publisher to publish messages to the stream:

```
$ python ch5_aws_publisher.py
{'prop': '104', 'timestamp': '1636163474', 'thing_id': 'aa-bb'}
{'prop': '45', 'timestamp': '1636163480', 'thing_id': 'aa-bb'}
...
```

8. We can now observe the messages on the subscriber terminal:

```
{'Records': [{'SequenceNumber': '49623659473219395665727562053704988803\
010408000553746434', 'ApproximateArrivalTimestamp': datetime.datetime(2\
021, 11, 5, 18, 51, 45, 301000, tzinfo=tzlocal()), 'Data': b'{"prop": "\
98", "timestamp": "1636163505", "thing_id": "aa-bb"}', 'PartitionKey': \
'aa-bb'}], 'NextShardIterator': 'AAAAAAAAAAEmWaOi5OTtl/PbyDFSnVQJF13WiS\
wPLNKnjT8/FmNicqRc/OKfXnXqMrUdjOsXzstfBrr8mnmvfyztMEVQSD1pv0L7GfZuZ5Vvr\
EP/5pQfcqMRFSUFMPE+KPK1Mv8JUZbYRTQ91DdWOvwdAGREr7peKxYsk9egNDgyT6Sj4LGc\
QAHWyGKiEQl31L/sJZ5QUIjpjZv8RCwhfGeErwrZP5SsZ/ACu/HAfmcdTBohQUb2RrK1a2q\
oXNP1NH1h4jEsL80=', 'MillisBehindLatest': 0, 'ResponseMetadata': {'Requ\
estId': 'd8524aa1-62ae-7748-81ad-ab52a6f07546', 'HTTPStatusCode': 200, \
'HTTPHeaders': {'x-amzn-requestid': 'd8524aa1-62ae-7748-81ad-ab52a6f075\
46', 'x-amz-id-2': '5Fw8UH2f+Z/EZ8dsmKfhCcVQNqhRqxcW0k+0UkcdkZWaL4ZglYb\
++s2IJIexgKK/3W2u7ZppQP7tR9LX33XnWdHHJOT9zdPGM+ZCCgedCBM=', 'date': 'Sa\
t, 06 Nov 2021 01:51:47 GMT', 'content-type': 'application/x-amz-json-1\
.1', 'content-length': '569'}, 'RetryAttempts': 0}}
...
```


Kinesis is a quick and convenient way to integrate streaming services into our workflow. Before the launch of Amazon MSK, this was the only way to utilize a managed streaming service in AWS. There are minor differences between Kafka and Kinesis, mainly in the terminology. However, the basic concepts are similar between the two services.

Kinesis is easy to launch and use. We can use it one topic at a time. I see the service as a potential transitional step from proof-of-concept to a full Kafka cluster. Of course, if we only have a few topics, we can continue using Kinesis until they do not fit our needs anymore. The downside, of course, is the need to change the code when we do switch from Kinesis to full a Kafka cluster.

Azure Event Hub

Azure Event Hubs is a data streaming platform. It is very similar to Kafka in terms of having publishers and subscribers. Azure Event Hub is unique in terms of its support for compatibility for Apache Kafka. However, Event Hub uses different terminology to describe its Kafka-equivalent cousins.

- Kafka Cluster = Event Hub Namespace
- Kafka Topic = Event Hub
- Kafka Partition = Event Hub Partition
- Kafka Consumer Group = Event Hub Consumer Group
- Kafka Offset = Event Hub Offset

There are also some differences between the two, such as the asynchronous messaging options in Azure. For more information, please take a look at Use Azure Event Hubs from Apache Kafka applications[47].

Azure Event Hub Example

Much like AWS, creating an Event in Azure Event Hub consist of Azure resource management as well as Event Hub-specific steps. We will begin by setting up Azure CLI before moving on to work with Event Hub.

Two great resources to consult are:

Event Hubs Quick Start Guide[48] and the
Event Hub Python Example[49].

[47]https://docs.microsoft.com/en-us/azure/event-hubs/event-hubs-for-kafka-ecosystem-overview
[48]https://docs.microsoft.com/en-us/azure/event-hubs/event-hubs-quickstart-cli
[49]https://docs.microsoft.com/en-us/azure/event-hubs/event-hubs-python-get-started-send

Ready? Let's get started.

1. We will need to install Azure CLI first:

```
$ curl -sL https://aka.ms/InstallAzureCLIDeb | sudo bash
```

2. We will set up Azure CLI credentials via the *az login* command. This will redirect us to the Azure web portal for authentication. Once authenticated, we will receive a token to be entered into the command line:

```
$ az login
```

3. Azure differentiates projects via *resource groups*. We can either create a new resource group or use an existing one. Here we will create a new resource group:

```
$ az group create --name eventhub-test --location eastus
```

4. From there, we will create an *Event Hub namespace*. A namespace is similar to a self-contained bubble. It separates one Event Hub from another:

```
$ az eventhubs namespace create --name eventhub-test --resource-group e\
venthub-test -l eastus
```

5. We can now create an event hub event within the namespace:

```
$ az eventhubs eventhub create --name test-event --resource-group event\
hub-test --namespace-name eventhub-test
```

6. Let's install the Azure Event Hub Python packages:

Remember to activate your Python virtual environment.

```
$ pip install azure-eventhub
$ pip install azure-eventhub-checkpointstoreblob-aio
```

7. We can now create a publisher, *ch5_azure_publisher.py*:

Azure requires a connection string to be entered into the script. This connection string contains the location of the resources as well as user credentials. As explained by this document[50], the string can be found under 'shared access policies':

Figure 5.3 Azure Event Hub Connection String

Below is the content of the publisher script.

[50] https://docs.microsoft.com/en-us/azure/event-hubs/event-hubs-get-connection-string

```
# Example from https://docs.microsoft.com/en-us/azure/event-hubs/event-\
hubs-python-get-started-send
import asyncio
from azure.eventhub.aio import EventHubProducerClient
from azure.eventhub import EventData

async def run():
    # Create a producer client to send messages to the event hub.
    # Specify a connection string to your event hubs namespace and
    # the event hub name.
    producer = EventHubProducerClient.from_connection_string(conn_str="\
Endpoint=sb://eventhub-test.servicebus.windows.net/;SharedAccessKeyName\
=manage-event-hub;SharedAccessKey=<key>;EntityPath=test-event", eventhu\
b_name="test-event")
    async with producer:
        # Create a batch.
        event_data_batch = await producer.create_batch()

        # Add events to the batch.
        event_data_batch.add(EventData('First event '))
        event_data_batch.add(EventData('Second event'))
        event_data_batch.add(EventData('Third event'))

        # Send the batch of events to the event hub.
        await producer.send_batch(event_data_batch)

loop = asyncio.get_event_loop()
loop.run_until_complete(run())
```

One thing to note from the script is it uses the Python 3 asyncio[51] library. Asyncio is a library to write concurrent code using the async/await syntax. This allows for higher performance by sending the events without waiting for the response before sending the next event. We should also take note that the events are put into a batch before sending.

[51] https://docs.python.org/3/library/asyncio.html

If we would like to preserve the ordering of events, we can send the events to a specific partition. In the next step, we will create a consumer for our event topic.

8. Let's create the subscriber script, *ch5_azure_subscriber.py*:

```
# Example from https://docs.microsoft.com/en-us/azure/event-hubs/event-\
hubs-python-get-started-send
import asyncio
from azure.eventhub.aio import EventHubConsumerClient
from azure.eventhub.extensions.checkpointstoreblobaio import BlobCheckp\
ointStore


async def on_event(partition_context, event):
    # Print the event data.
    print("Received the event: \"{}\" from the partition with ID: \"{}\\
"".format(event.body_as_str(encoding='UTF-8'), partition_context.partit\
ion_id))

    # Update the checkpoint so that the program doesn't read the events
    # that it has already read when you run it next time.
    await partition_context.update_checkpoint(event)

async def main():
    client = EventHubConsumerClient.from_connection_string("Endpoint=sb\
://eventhub-test.servicebus.windows.net/;SharedAccessKeyName=manage-eve\
nt-hub;SharedAccessKey=<key>;EntityPath=test-event", consumer_group="$D\
efault", eventhub_name="test-event")
    async with client:
        # Call the receive method. Read from the beginning of the parti\
tion (starting_position: "-1")
        await client.receive(on_event=on_event, starting_position="-1")

if __name__ == '__main__':
    loop = asyncio.get_event_loop()
```

```
    # Run the main method.
    loop.run_until_complete(main())
```

Again, the subscriber script uses the Python aysncio library to allow better performance. One thing to note is the usage of checkout. This is analogous to the Kafka consumer offset. In the script, we manually update the position of the processed message by updating the checkpoint.

9. As we have done before, let's start subscriber on a terminal and let it run:

```
$ python ch5_azure_subscriber.py
```

10. We can start publisher to publish events:

```
$ python ch5_azure_publisher.py
```

11. Now, let's observe the events on the subscriber terminal:

```
Received the event: "First event " from the partition with ID: "0"
Received the event: "Second event" from the partition with ID: "0"
Received the event: "Third event" from the partition with ID: "0"
...
```

You might be thinking: "Didn't Azure list compatibility with Kafka?" One thing we did not mention is the Event Hubs pricing structure. Azure Event Hubs are broken into different tiers: basic, standard, premium, and dedicated. The services offered, including Kafka compatibility, differs between the different tiers.

- Azure Event Hubs Pricing[52]

[52]https://azure.microsoft.com/en-us/pricing/details/event-hubs/

Kafka compatibility is offered in the standard and above tiers. Besides Kafka integration, the standard tier offers additional features such as longer event retention and multiple consumer groups. At the time of writing, Event Hubs supports Apache Kafka 1.0.

More information on Event Hubs Kafka compatibility can be found:

- Apache Kafka Integration[53]
- Quickstart: Data Streaming with Event Hubs using the Kafka Protocol[54]
- Azure Event Hub schema registry[55]

In the next section, let's take a look at Google Cloud's Pub/Sub service.

Google Cloud Pub/Sub

Google Cloud Pub/Sub provides familiar terminology for us in terms of publishers and subscribers. Publishers can send messages to the Pub/Sub service, while the subscribers can receive events from the service. If you already use Google Cloud's big data services such as dataflow, BigQuery, and BigTable, the Pub/Sub service would complement them by allowing multiple clients to subscribe to the same event simultaneously.

Pub/Sub service differs from Kafka in terms of parallel processing. Pub-/Sub offers per-message parallelism instead of Kafka's partition-based parallel processing. This means we do not need to improve the number of partitions in order to increase performance.

There are some core concepts for the Pub/Sub service:

[53]https://docs.microsoft.com/en-us/azure/event-hubs/event-hubs-faq#apache-kafka-integration
[54]https://docs.microsoft.com/en-us/azure/event-hubs/event-hubs-quickstart-kafka-enabled-event-hubs
[55]https://docs.microsoft.com/en-us/azure/event-hubs/create-schema-registry

- Topic: This is similar to Kafka's topics. We use topics to organize messages.
- Subscription: This is used for GCP service-to-service communication. Instead of a subscriber, a subscription is used for a service to receive messages.
- Message and Message attribute: The message is the data being transmitted. The message can also include attributes in key-value pairs. The attributes are used easily identify the messages.
- Publisher / Subscriber: This is what we would imagine them to be. The publisher pushes the message to the service while the subscriber pulls the messages.
- Acknowledgement: This is similar to the committed offset we have seen in the Kafka service.

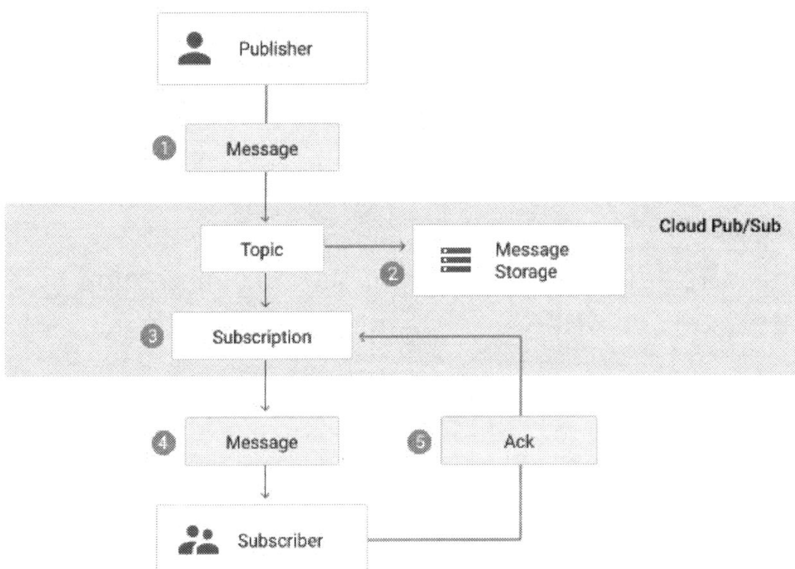

Figure 5.4 Google Cloud Pub/Sub Overview

Let's take a look at a quick GCP Pub/Sub Python example.

GCP Pub/Sub Python Example

Before we can launch any service in Google Cloud, we need to create a new project or use an existing one. I will create a new project for this example:

1. The new project is named *pubsub-testing*:

Figure 5.5 Google Cloud Project

2. Enable the necessary API for the project, in this case, Pub/Sub API:

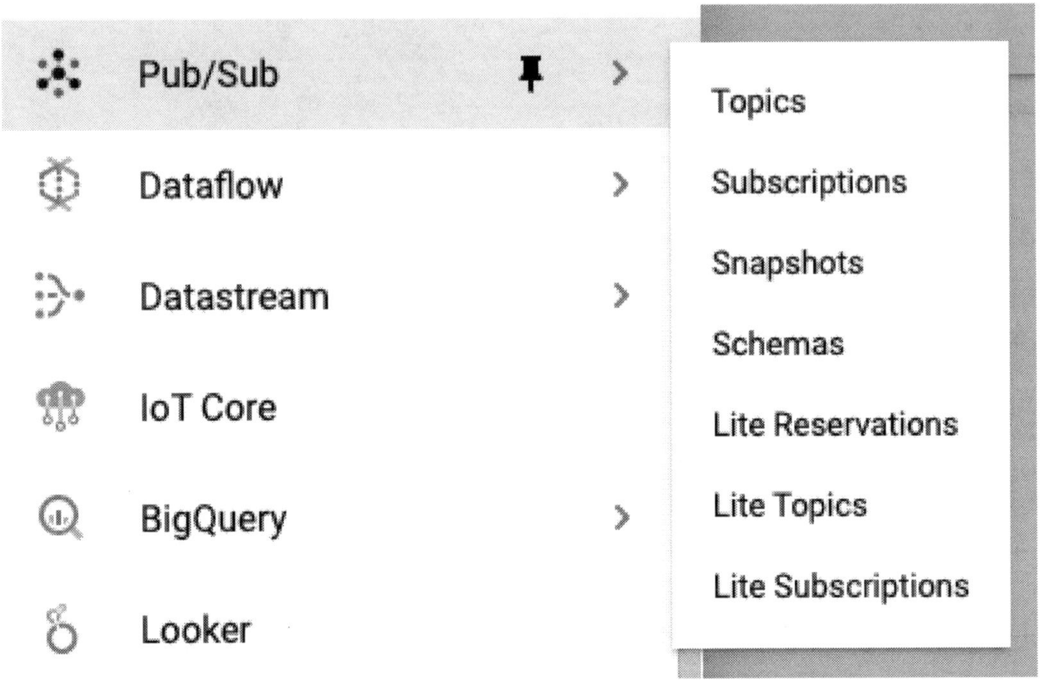

Figure 5.6 Enable Pub/Sub API

3. We will create a service account for the project:

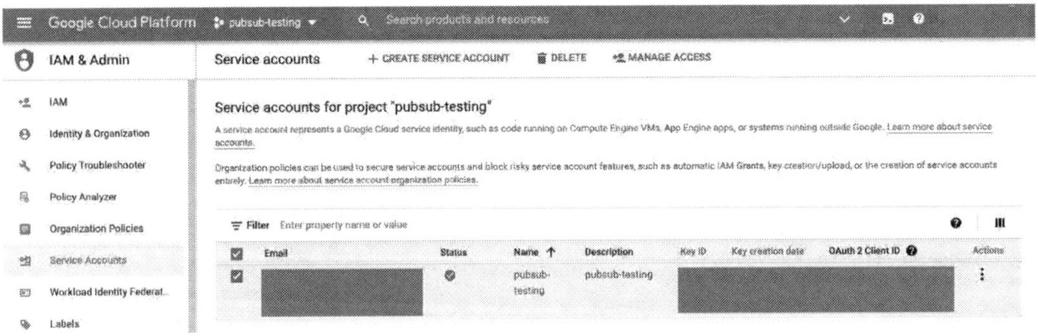

Figure 5.7 Google Cloud Service Account

4. Let's create an API key for the service account. The key will be a JSON file, which we will download and save onto our host. We will export the content of this file in the specific environment variable named

GOOGLE_APPLICATION_CREDENTIALS:

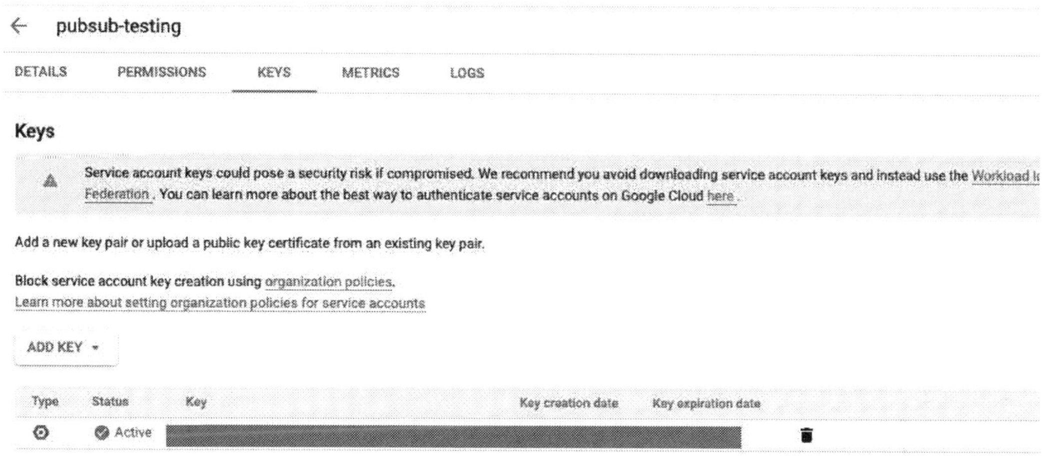

Figure 5.8 GCP API Key

```
$ export GOOGLE_APPLICATION_CREDENTIALS="<path to json file>"
```

5. Let's install the Google Cloud SDK:

> Follow the instruction on GCP Cloud SDK Quickstart[56] to install the SDK on various platforms.

```
$ gcloud --version
Google Cloud SDK 363.0.0
```

We will need to use *gcloud auth login* to enter the authentication credentials:

[56]https://cloud.google.com/sdk/docs/quickstart

```
$ gcloud auth login
<follow the onscreen steps>
```

We will change to the project that we created:

```
$ gcloud config set project <project id>
```

The following steps are specific to the Pub/Sub service, taken from the GCP Pub/Sub Quick Start Page[57]:

1. We will install the Google Cloud Pub/Sub client library:

```
$ pip install --upgrade google-cloud-pubsub
```

2. The next step is to create a topic, *test-topic*:

```
$ gcloud pubsub topics create test-topic
```

3. Let's create the publisher, *ch5_gcp_publisher.py*:

```
from google.cloud import pubsub_v1

project_id = "pubsub-testing-<id>"
topic_id = "test-topic"

publisher = pubsub_v1.PublisherClient()
# The `topic_path` method creates a fully qualified identifier
# in the form `projects/{project_id}/topics/{topic_id}`
topic_path = publisher.topic_path(project_id, topic_id)

for n in range(1, 10):
    data = f"Message number {n}"
```

[57] https://cloud.google.com/pubsub/docs/quickstart-client-libraries

```
    # Data must be a bytestring
    data = data.encode("utf-8")
    # When you publish a message, the client returns a future.
    future = publisher.publish(topic_path, data)
    print(future.result())

print(f"Published messages to {topic_path}.")
```

The script is similar to what we have used before. The response for the message produced is called a *future* in GCP.

4. Let's create a subscription to the topic:

```
$ gcloud pubsub subscriptions create test-sub --topic test-topic
```

5. Let's create the subscriber, *ch5_gcp_subscribder.py*:

```
from concurrent.futures import TimeoutError
from google.cloud import pubsub_v1

project_id = "pubsub-testing-<id>"
subscription_id = "test-sub"
# Number of seconds the subscriber should listen for messages
timeout = 5.0

subscriber = pubsub_v1.SubscriberClient()
# The `subscription_path` method creates a fully qualified identifier
# in the form `projects/{project_id}/subscriptions/{subscription_id}`
subscription_path = subscriber.subscription_path(project_id, subscripti\
on_id)

def callback(message: pubsub_v1.subscriber.message.Message) -> None:
    print(f"Received {message}.")
    message.ack()

```

```
streaming_pull_future = subscriber.subscribe(subscription_path, callbac\
k=callback)
print(f"Listening for messages on {subscription_path}..\n")

# Wrap subscriber in a 'with' block to automatically call close() when \
done.
with subscriber:
    try:
        # When `timeout` is not set, result() will block indefinitely,
        # unless an exception is encountered first.
        streaming_pull_future.result(timeout=timeout)
    except TimeoutError:
        streaming_pull_future.cancel()  # Trigger the shutdown.
        streaming_pull_future.result()  # Block until the shutdown is c\
omplete.
```

The subscriber script provides a callback function for Pub/Sub to contact when the message is pushed to the subscriber. The callback function also provides message acknowledgment back to Pub/Sub.

6. We will start the Subscriber process:

```
$ python ch5_gcp_subscriber.py
```

7. Let's publish messages to the topic:

```
$ python ch5_gcp_publisher.py
3333289788861597
3333305112028909
3333301553296156
3333303808694942
3333300923525483
3333306271607426
3333295865262744
3333295110730825
3333295329446541
Published messages to projects/pubsub-testing-<id>/topics/test-topic.
```

8. We can now observe the output on the subscriber:

```
Listening for messages on projects/pubsub-testing-331300/subscriptions/\
test-sub..

Received Message {
  data: b'Message number 1'
  ordering_key: ''
  attributes: {}
}.
Received Message {
  data: b'Message number 5'
  ordering_key: ''
  attributes: {}
}.
Received Message {
  data: b'Message number 9'
  ordering_key: ''
  attributes: {}
}.
...
```

As we can see, the GCP Pub/Sub process is similar to the Kafka process with minor differences. Outside of the Google Cloud-specific process, most of the difference is using a different Python client library and syntax changes. In my opinion, the biggest difference in GCP is its wide support for Big Data. The Pub/Sub is a complimentary service to the other Big Data analytical services GCP provides.

Conclusion

This chapter looked at the top 3 public cloud providers' adaptation of the data streaming concepts. The services have various similarities and differences between themselves and the Kafka services. They tend to be providers specific, with some providers open for more Kafka support.

In my opinion, they are good options to choose from when we are moving away from a lab environment but not yet ready to manage our own Kafka cluster. As with any trade-off, if we do decide to use them, we need to be ready to rewrite our code in the future if we do decide to move to a full Kafka cluster at a later time.

In the next chapter, we will dive deeper into the various use cases for Kafka in network engineering.

Chapter 6. Network Operations with Kafka

We now have a good understanding of Kafka's concept and operations. It is time to look at some practical examples. We are particularly interested in how Kafka can be integrated into network management. There are several ways we can incorporate Kafka into our workflow. For instance, we can use Kafka to manage and enhance data, such as logs, or we can use Kafka as an intermediary component to smooth out the data stream.

Some of the network use cases include:

- Cisco Engineering Kafka for Secure Autonomous Operation[58]
- CIsco's Real-Time Ingestion Architecture with Kafka and Druid[59]
- Nanog 65: Monitor BGP using open source OpenBMP and Apache Kafka[60]

This chapter will build upon our previous producer and consumer code and gradually work out a way toward Kafka connectors. Toward the end, we will also use Elasticsearch as our Kafka output destination.

[58] https://video.cisco.com/video/6258279442001
[59] https://imply.io/videos/ciscos-real-time-ingestion-architecture-with-kafka-and-druid
[60] https://www.youtube.com/watch?v=YsupfSHKSqw

Install Docker

For the last example in this chapter, we will use the popular Elastic Stack[61] to illustrate Kafka and Kafka Connectors. To do so with a limited amount of resources, we will leverage Docker and containers on our existing Linux host. Both Docker containers and Elastic Stack are popular open-source projects. However, they can feel complex in the beginning. I want to provide realistic examples of how Kafka can be used in real-world use cases, but neither project is required to learn about Kafka.

Please feel free to skip the Docker and Elastic Stack installation section if you do not want to perform the last example.

> ⚠ Again, both Elasticsearch and Docker are entire book-worthy topics in their own rights. Going deeper into either subject is outside the scope of this book. However, please do feel free to glance over them first and decide if you would like to try out the examples in this chapter.

Docker containers are like small virtual machines running inside of our Virtual Machine. As such, we should increase the VM's resources if we can. In particular, we should allocate as much RAM as we can. For the following examples running two containers and Kafka on the same server, I ran the setup with 8GB of RAM.

Following the installation instruction[62] from the Docker documentation, here are the steps to install Docker Engine on the Ubuntu host:

[61] https://www.elastic.co/guide/en/elasticsearch/reference/current/index.html
[62] https://docs.docker.com/engine/install/ubuntu/

```
$ sudo apt-get remove docker docker-engine docker.io containerd runc
$ sudo apt-get install ca-certificates curl gnupg lsb-release
$ curl -fsSL https://download.docker.com/linux/ubuntu/gpg | sudo gpg --\
dearmor -o /usr/share/keyrings/docker-archive-keyring.gpg
$ echo \
>   "deb [arch=$(dpkg --print-architecture) signed-by=/usr/share/keyrin\
gs/docker-archive-keyring.gpg] https://download.docker.com/linux/ubuntu\
 \
>   $(lsb_release -cs) stable" | sudo tee /etc/apt/sources.list.d/docke\
r.list > /dev/null
$ sudo apt update
$ sudo apt-get install docker-ce docker-ce-cli containerd.io
```

As a reminder, we can start/stop/remove docker images with the following commands. By default, the commands require root privileges:

```
sudo docker ps
sudo docker stop <container id>
sudo docker start <container id>
sudo rm <container id>
```

We can run containers in detached mode with the *–detach* option, which means the container will run as background processes. This is what I usually do when everything is working fine. But in a lab or during learning, I typically wish to see the launch and error messages (if any). In the following examples, I do not use the detached option by design.

Install Elasticsearch

Elastic search provides instructions to install and run Elasticsearch in a container[63]. The summary is listed below. In Elasticsearch, we need

[63] https://www.elastic.co/guide/en/elasticsearch/reference/current/docker.html

port 9200 for the Elasticsearch process. Port 9300 is used for inter-node communication between Elasticsearch nodes. Port 9300 is optional for us since we only run it in a single-node setup. When we run the containers, we will map our local VM ports to the two containers.

We will pull the image down first, then create a docker network:

```
$ sudo docker pull docker.elastic.co/elasticsearch/elasticsearch:7.15.1
$ sudo docker network create elastic
```

Once the image is downloaded, we can launch the service. The first time we run the container, it will take a while to run:

```
$ sudo docker run --name es01-test --net elastic -p 9200:9200 -p 9300:9\
300 -e "discovery.type=single-node" docker.elastic.co/elasticsearch/ela\
sticsearch:7.15.1
```

We can check the status of the docker image:

```
$ sudo docker ps
CONTAINER ID   IMAGE                                                  C\
OMMAND                  CREATED           STATUS           PORTS          \
                                                                          \
  NAMES
401165afc42e   docker.elastic.co/elasticsearch/elasticsearch:7.15.1   "\
/bin/tini -- /usr/l…"   40 seconds ago   Up 40 seconds   0.0.0.0:9200->\
9200/tcp, :::9200->9200/tcp, 0.0.0.0:9300->9300/tcp, :::9300->9300/tcp \
  es01-test
```

We can test the operation of Elasticsearch by curling to port 9200. Notice we curl to the localhost, but the traffic is passed to the Elasticsearch container:

```
$ curl localhost:9200
{
  "name" : "401165afc42e",
  "cluster_name" : "docker-cluster",
  "cluster_uuid" : "ClM_DAeHTuazLaPtK6QTqw",
  "version" : {
    "number" : "7.15.1",
    "build_flavor" : "default",
    "build_type" : "docker",
    "build_hash" : "83c34f456ae29d60e94d886e455e6a3409bba9ed",
    "build_date" : "2021-10-07T21:56:19.031608185Z",
    "build_snapshot" : false,
    "lucene_version" : "8.9.0",
    "minimum_wire_compatibility_version" : "6.8.0",
    "minimum_index_compatibility_version" : "6.0.0-beta1"
  },
  "tagline" : "You Know, for Search"
}
```

We need to have Elasticsearch running before we can move on to Kibana, which is the frontend visualization and management component for the stack.

Install Kibana

Kibana can be installed following the online instruction[64]. The default port for Kibana is 5601. We will follow the familiar pattern of pulling down the image first, then launch the service and map the port to the localhost:

[64]https://www.elastic.co/guide/en/kibana/current/docker.html

```
$ sudo docker pull docker.elastic.co/kibana/kibana:7.15.1
$ sudo docker run --name kib01-test --net elastic -p 5601:5601 -e "ELAS\
TICSEARCH_HOSTS=http://es01-test:9200" docker.elastic.co/kibana/kibana:\
7.15.1
```

Kibana has a dependency on Elasticsearch. If we see the following error, the Elasticsearch node is not discovered by Kibana:

```
{"type":"log","@timestamp":"2021-11-06T15:03:44+00:00","tags":["error",\
"savedobjects-service"],"pid":1219,"message":"Unable to retrieve versio\
n information from Elasticsearch nodes. getaddrinfo ENOTFOUND elastic-t\
est"}
```

When we see the following message, Kibana is ready:

```
{"type":"log","@timestamp":"2021-11-06T15:21:00+00:00","tags":["info","\
status"],"pid":1219,"message":"Kibana is now available (was degraded)"}
```

We can now point our browser to 'kafka-1:5601':

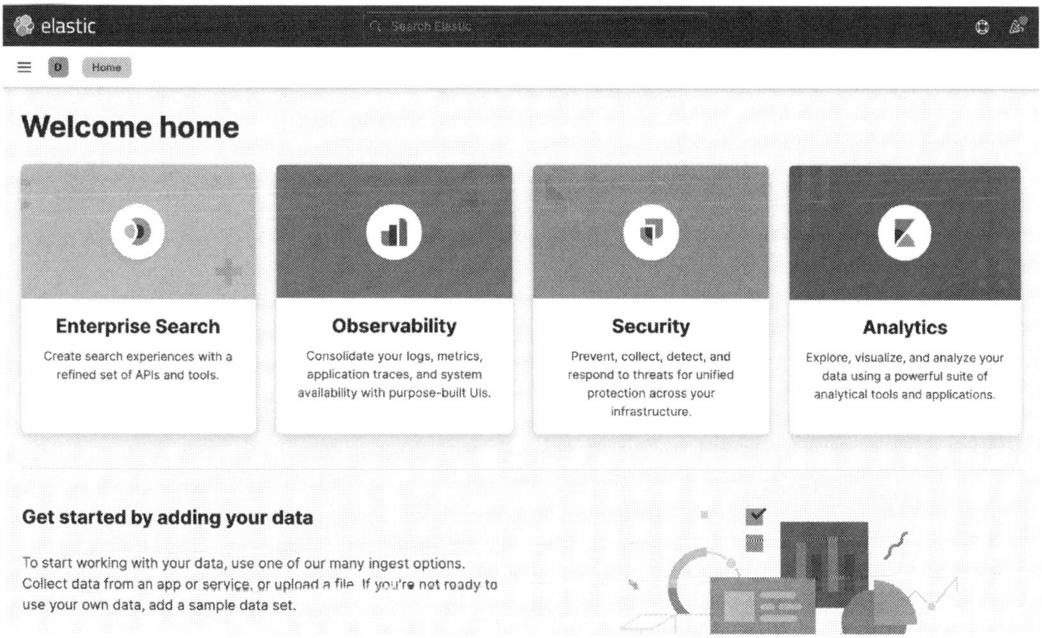

Figure 6.1 Kibana Home

By default, Kibana provides multiple sets of external test data. I typically like to import a few sets of data to make sure the setup is working:

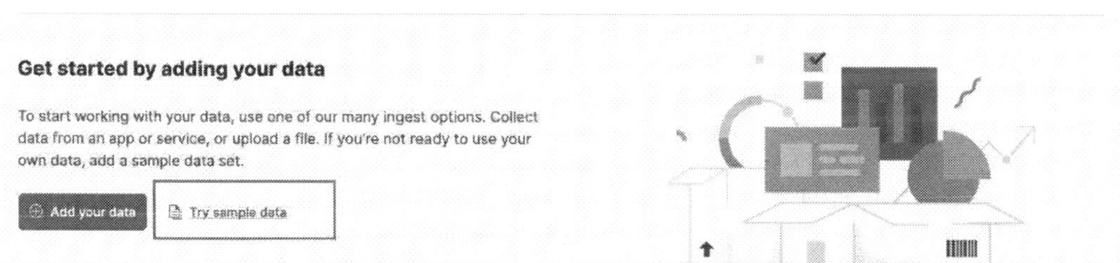

Figure 6.2 Kibana Test Data

We can choose from a few sets of data:

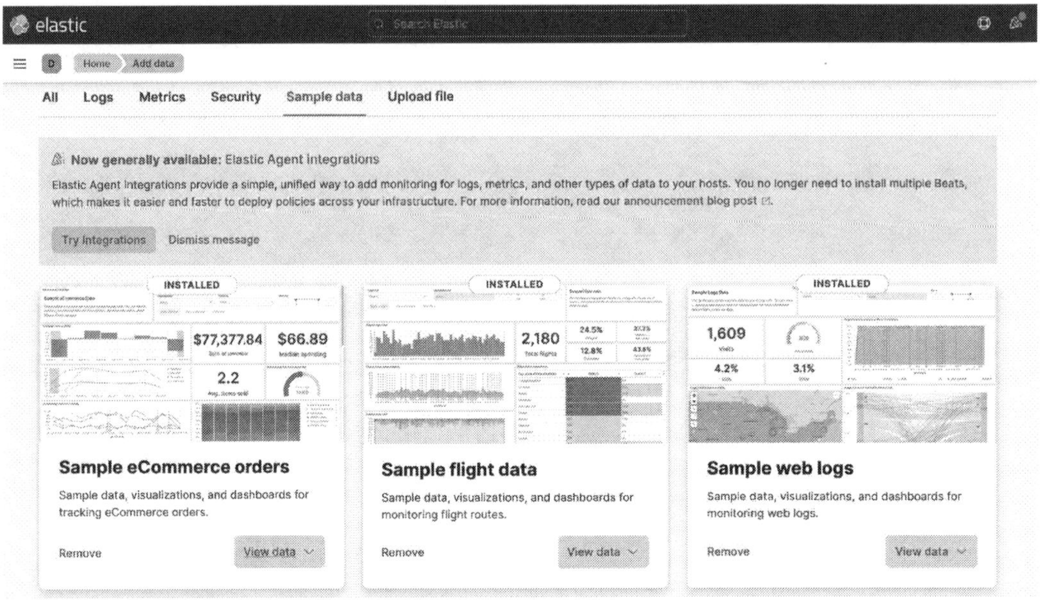

Figure 6.3 Kibana Sample Data Sets

If you came from an older version of Elasticsearch or Kibana, you might be wondering where the Discovery panel went. In Kibana 7.15, it is under Analytics:

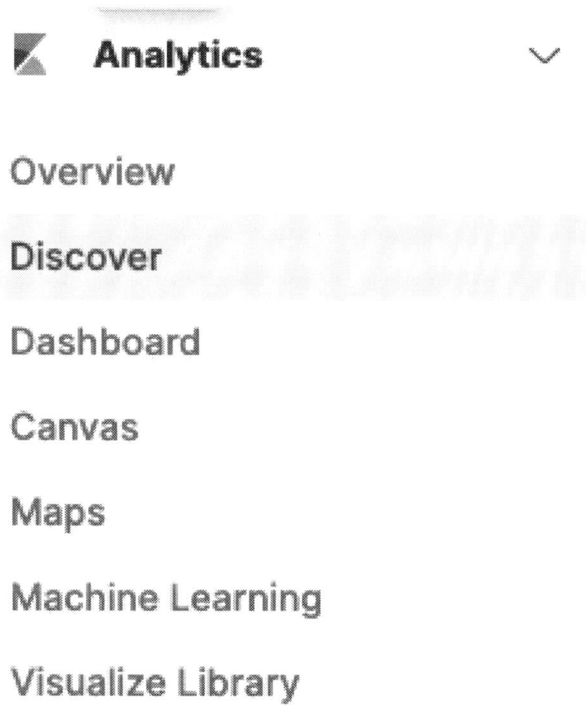

Figure 6.4 Kibana Discover

If you are interested in exploring Kibana further, please consult the Kibana administrative guide[65].

By default, *xpack.security.enable* is set to true, and a pop-up will be displayed if you do not set up xpack.security. If you are ok with turning security off in a lab, to stop security warnings, you can stop the Elasticsearch container and re-run it with security disabled:

[65] https://www.elastic.co/guide/en/kibana/current/index.html

```
$ sudo docker stop es01-test
$ sudo docker stop kib01-test
$ sudo docker rm es01-test
$ sudo docker run --name es01-test --net elastic -p 9200:9200 -p 9300:9\
300 -e "discovery.type=single-node" -e "xpack.security.enabled=false" d\
ocker.elastic.co/elasticsearch/elasticsearch:7.15.1
```

Ok, let us start to work on some of the examples. We will gradually work from a few relatively simple measures to a more complicated workflow involving Kafka and Elasticsearch.

Network Data Feed

We will begin by using NXAPI to query network device information and feed them into a Kafka topic. To use NXAPI, we will need to turn on the feature as well as perform some related configuration tasks:

```
lax-cor-r1(config)# feature nxapi
lax-cor-r1(config)# nxapi http port 80
lax-cor-r1(config)# nxapi sandbox
nyc-cor-r1(config)# feature nxapi
nyc-cor-r1(config)# nxapi http port 80
nyc-cor-r1(config)# nxapi sandbox
```

We also need to have local users who have administrative rights, such as below:

```
username cisco password 5 $1$Nk7ZkwH0$fyiRmMMfIheqE3BqvcL0C1  role netw\
ork-opera
tor
username cisco role network-admin
username cisco passphrase  lifetime 99999 warntime 14 gracetime 3
```

We will be using the Python requests package to make HTTP calls to Nexus devices. Let's install it before we forget:

```
$ pip install requests
```

We will create a topic, *ch6_topic_show_ver*, for this first example. Let's use the familiar *kafka-topic.sh* to do so:

```
$ kafka-topics.sh --zookeeper 127.0.0.1:2181 --topic ch6_topic_show_ver\
 --create --partitions 3 --replication-factor 1
```

We can use the following script, *ch6_show_version_producer.py*, to query the Nexus devices with a structured data back containing what we would typically see in 'show version' output. We created a function to better separate that function from the rest of the code.

We also created a function as a callback to be passed in the producer method since we are producing the message asynchronously. Note that we are using 'utf-16' encoding to create message keys. This is just with some trial and error that I found to be better suited for key ByteArray generation.

```
#!/usr/bin/env python3

from confluent_kafka import Producer
import requests
import json
from datetime import datetime

devices = {
    'lax-cor-r1': {'ip': '192.168.2.50'},
    'nyc-cor-r1': {'ip': '192.168.2.60'}
}

def show_version(host, username, password):
    url = f"http://{host}/ins"
    myheaders={'content-type':'application/json-rpc'}
    payload=[
    {
        "jsonrpc": "2.0",
        "method": "cli",
        "params": {
        "cmd": "show version",
        "version": 1.2
        },
        "id": 1
    }
    ]
    response = requests.post(url,data=json.dumps(payload), headers=myhe\
aders, auth=(username, password)).json()

    return response['result']['body']


# Provides call back for Kafka delivery response
delivered_records = 0
def acked(err, msg):
    global delivered_records
```

```
    """Delivery report handler called on
    successful or failed delivery of message
    """
    if err is not None:
        print("Failed to deliver message: %s: %s" % (str(msg), str(err)\
))
    else:
        delivered_records += 1
        print("Produced record to topic {} partition [{}] @ offset {}"
            .format(msg.topic(), msg.partition(), msg.offset()))


if __name__ == "__main__":
    conf = {'bootstrap.servers': "kafka-1:9092", 'client.id': '1'}
    producer = Producer(conf)
    # query_results = []
    for device in devices:
        # Query for Device Information
        print(f"Querying Information on {device}")
        ip = devices[device]['ip']
        result = show_version(ip, 'cisco', 'cisco')

        # construct record
        record_key = device.encode("utf-16")
        record_value = json.dumps({
            'Time': str(datetime.now()),
            'Output': result
        })

        # produce to Kafka
        producer.produce("ch6_topic_show_ver", key=record_key, value=re\
cord_value, on_delivery=acked)
        producer.poll(0)

    producer.flush()
```

Most of the code to produce messages is in the main function. We have already seen this portion a few times, so I won't spend too much time explaining it. To subscribe to the topic and display the version information, we will construct the following consumer code, *ch6_show_-version_consumer.py*. Since we encode the key with 'utf-16' we will need to decode it as such.

```
from confluent_kafka import Consumer
import json

conf = {'bootstrap.servers': 'kafka-1:9092', 'group.id': 'ch6_consumer_\
group_1'}

consumer = Consumer(conf)
consumer.subscribe(['ch6_topic_show_ver'])
try:
    while True:
        msg = consumer.poll(timeout=1.0)
        if msg is None:
            continue
        elif msg.error():
            print('error: {}'.format(msg.error()))
        else:
            record_key = msg.key().decode('utf-16')
            record_value = msg.value()
            print(f'Device: {record_key}, Version:', json.loads(record_\
value)['Output']['sys_ver_str'])

except KeyboardInterrupt:
    pass
finally:
    consumer.close()
```

When we run the producer, we are expected to see the querying information when we loop thru the two devices, as well as the callback output for offset and partition information from the callback function.

```
$ python ch6_show_version_producer.py
Querying Information on lax-cor-r1
Querying Information on nyc-cor-r1
Produced record to topic ch6_topic_show_ver partition [0] @ offset 0
Produced record to topic ch6_topic_show_ver partition [2] @ offset 0
```

On the consumer end, we should see the output for the device as well as the software version:

```
$ python ch6_show_version_consumer.py
Device: nyc-cor-r1, Version: 7.3(0)D1(1)
Device: lax-cor-r1, Version: 7.3(0)D1(1)
```

At this point, you might be wondering why we are using Kafka at all. The same script could have just queried the device and displayed the output. Remember, Kafka is used for scalability and separation of concerns. In simple tasks, it is almost always an overkill. But when we look closer, there are many benefits of using Kafka:

- We can have multiple producers querying the network devices. Each producer can handle a 'micro' segment of the network or device such as spine-only or leaf-only row. We can also separate the tasks by know-how. For example, we can have another producer handling all IOS devices or Juniper devices, depending on engineer expertise.
- We do not need to use the same language for writing producers. Kafka provides many different SDKs for different languages. If our team member decides to use Go or C#, they are free to do so.
- If there are multiple teams required to use the same network output. Multiple consumer groups can be used. The Kafka cluster will be in charge of the ordering and delivery.

- By having Kafka handle the messages, we do not need to put more overhead on the network devices when more group needs the same information. We query the network device once regardless of how many times the message is being consumed by different groups.
- The data is retained and persisted by the Kafka cluster for a period of time. We do not have to worry about data collectors or consumers going offline for a period of time.

Another benefit of using Kafka is the fact that we can start to enrich the data by adding more information and transforming the data. Let's take a look at an example in the next section.

Network Data Pipeline

In the following example, we will take messages from a topic, transform them, then push them to another topic. Here is the general process:

Producer for Topic 1 -> Consumer Topic 1 -> Enhance Topic 1 Message -> Produce to New Topic 2

In particular, here is what we will do:

- We will take a 'show inventory' output from the devices.
- We will match the device from an external CSV file that contains the address of the device.
- We will produce a new record with the additional information.
- We will push the new record to a new topic.

Let us create an inventory file with device addresses, *ch6_hardware_-data.csv*. This can also be a text file, database query, or anything else that is external:

```
hostname, address
nyc-cor-r1, 111 Steady Rd., New York, NY 11111
lax-cor-r1, 100 Watcher St., Los Angeles, CA 22222
```

For this example, we will create two new topics, *ch6_topic_show_inventory* and *ch6_topic_hardware*:

```
$ kafka-topics.sh --zookeeper 127.0.0.1:2181 --topic ch6_topic_show_inv\
entory --create --partitions 3 --replication-factor 1
$ kafka-topics.sh --zookeeper 127.0.0.1:2181 --topic ch6_topic_datacent\
er_hardware --create --partitions 3 --replication-factor 1
```

The producer of 'show inventory' script, *ch6_show_inventory_producer.py*, is very similar to the previous 'show version' script, except for the use of 'show inventory' for the query. Therefore I only paste in the difference below:

```
...
def show_inventory(host, username, password):
    url = f"http://{host}/ins"
    myheaders={'content-type':'application/json-rpc'}
    payload=[
    {
        "jsonrpc": "2.0",
        "method": "cli",
        "params": {
        "cmd": "show inventory",
        "version": 1.2
        },
        "id": 1
    }
    ]
    response = requests.post(url,data=json.dumps(payload), headers=myhe\
aders, auth=(username, password)).json()
```

```

    return response['result']['body']
...
```

Here is an example of the output when the script runs:

```
...
Querying Information on nyc-cor-r1
{'TABLE_inv': {'ROW_inv': [{'name': '"Chassis"', 'desc': '"NX-OSv Chass\
is "', 'productid': 'N7K-C7018', 'vendorid': 'V00', 'serialnum': 'TB000\
06B77B'}, {'name': '"Slot 1"', 'desc': '"NX-OSv Supervisor Module"', 'p\
roductid': 'N7K-SUP1', 'vendorid': 'V00', 'serialnum': 'TM00006B77B'}, \
{'name': '"Slot 2"', 'desc': '"NX-OSv Ethernet Module"', 'productid': '\
N7K-F248XP-25', 'vendorid': 'V00', 'serialnum': 'TM00006B77C'}, {'name'\
: '"Slot 3"', 'desc': '"NX-OSv Ethernet Module"', 'productid': 'N7K-F24\
8XP-25', 'vendorid': 'V00', 'serialnum': 'TM00006B77D'}, {'name': '"Slo\
t 4"', 'desc': '"NX-OSv Ethernet Module"', 'productid': 'N7K-F248XP-25'\
, 'vendorid': 'V00', 'serialnum': 'TM00006B77E'}, {'name': '"Slot 33"',\
 'desc': '"NX-OSv Chassis Power Supply"', 'productid': '', 'vendorid': \
'V00', 'serialnum': ''}, {'name': '"Slot 35"', 'desc': '"NX-OSv Chassis\
 Fan Module"', 'productid': '', 'vendorid': 'V00', 'serialnum': ''}]}}
Produced record to topic ch6_topic_show_inventory partition [0] @ offse\
t 5
Produced record to topic ch6_topic_show_inventory partition [2] @ offse\
t 5
...
```

The new script, *ch6_multi_topic_consumer.py* utilizes several functions:

- Read the CSV file and puts the information in a dictionary format, with the key being the device hostname.
- Uses the same callback function as we have seen before to document the success and failure of the producer message to Kafka.
- It is acting as both a consumer and producer.

- It consumes messages from the topic *ch6_topic_show_inventory* and matches it up with the inventory address dictionary via the hostname.
- It adds timestamp, address, as well as the original 'show inventory' into a new record and pushes it to *ch6_topic_datacenter_hardware.*

Below is the content of the script:

```
import csv
from confluent_kafka import Consumer, Producer
import json
from datetime import datetime

def invenotry_information(csv_file):
    hardware_addresses = {}
    with open(csv_file) as csv_file:
        csv_reader = csv.reader(csv_file, delimiter=',')
        line_count = 0
        for row in csv_reader:
            # first line is header information
            if line_count == 0:
                pass
                line_count += 1
            else:
                hardware_addresses[row[0]] = {'street': row[1],
                                              'city': row[2],
                                              'zip_code': row[3]
                                             }
                line_count += 1
    return hardware_addresses

# Provides call back for Kafka delivery response
delivered_records = 0
def acked(err, msg):
    global delivered_records
```

```
    """Delivery report handler called on
    successful or failed delivery of message
    """
    if err is not None:
        print("Failed to deliver message: %s: %s" % (str(msg), str(err)\
))
    else:
        delivered_records += 1
        print("Produced record to topic {} partition [{}] @ offset {}"
            .format(msg.topic(), msg.partition(), msg.offset()))


if __name__ == "__main__":
    hardware_addresses = invenotry_information('ch6_hardware_data.csv')

    producer_conf = {'bootstrap.servers': "kafka-1:9092", 'client.id': \
'1'}
    producer = Producer(producer_conf)

    consumer_conf = {'bootstrap.servers': 'kafka-1:9092', 'group.id': '\
ch6_consumer_group_1'}
    consumer = Consumer(consumer_conf)
    consumer.subscribe(['ch6_topic_show_inventory'])
    try:
        while True:
            msg = consumer.poll(timeout=1.0)
            if msg is None:
                continue
            elif msg.error():
                print('error: {}'.format(msg.error()))
            else:
                record_key = msg.key().decode('utf-16')
                record_value = msg.value()
                # print(f'Device: {record_key}, Version:', json.loads(r\
ecord_value)['Output'])

```

```
                # construc new record
                # enhance with address record
                try:
                    address = hardware_addresses[record_key]
                except:
                    address = {}

                new_record_key = record_key.encode("utf-16")
                new_record_value = json.dumps({
                    'Time': str(datetime.now()),
                    'Address': address,
                    'Hardware': json.loads(record_value)['Output']
                })

                # produce to Kafka
                producer.produce("ch6_topic_datacenter_hardware", key=n\
ew_record_key, value=new_record_value, on_delivery=acked)
                producer.poll(0)

            producer.flush()

    except KeyboardInterrupt:
        pass
    finally:
        consumer.close()
```

We should start the consumer first so we can view the output when available:

```
$ python ch6_multi_topic_consumer.py
```

We can optionally start a console consumer for the second topic *ch6_-topic_datacenter_hardware* to validate the script's output:

```
$ kafka-console-consumer.sh --bootstrap-server 127.0.0.1:9092 --topic c\
h6_topic_datacenter_hardware --group consumer_group_1 --property parse.\
key=true
```

We will produce content to the first topic with the 'show inventory' from our devices:

```
$ python ch6_show_inventory_producer.py
```

On the output from the multi-topic consumer will show records produced via the callback function:

```
Produced record to topic ch6_topic_datacenter_hardware partition [0] @ \
offset 0
Produced record to topic ch6_topic_datacenter_hardware partition [2] @ \
offset 0
```

If we had started a console consumer for the second topic, we will be able to see the new records with the timestamp, address, and 'show inventory' data:


```
{"Time": "2021-11-07 06:44:24.055403", "Address": {"street": " 111 Stea\
dy Rd.", "city": " New York", "zip_code": " NY 11111"}, "Hardware": {"T\
ABLE_inv": {"ROW_inv": [{"name": "\"Chassis\"", "desc": "\"NX-OSv Chass\
is \"", "productid": "N7K-C7018", "vendorid": "V00", "serialnum": "TB00\
006B77B"}, {"name": "\"Slot 1\"", "desc": "\"NX-OSv Supervisor Module\"\
", "productid": "N7K-SUP1", "vendorid": "V00", "serialnum": "TM00006B77\
B"}, {"name": "\"Slot 2\"", "desc": "\"NX-OSv Ethernet Module\"", "prod\
uctid": "N7K-F248XP-25", "vendorid": "V00", "serialnum": "TM00006B77C"}\
, {"name": "\"Slot 3\"", "desc": "\"NX-OSv Ethernet Module\"", "product\
id": "N7K-F248XP-25", "vendorid": "V00", "serialnum": "TM00006B77D"}, {\
"name": "\"Slot 4\"", "desc": "\"NX-OSv Ethernet Module\"", "productid"\
: "N7K-F248XP-25", "vendorid": "V00", "serialnum": "TM00006B77E"}, {"na\
```

```
me": "\"Slot 33\"", "desc": "\"NX-OSv Chassis Power Supply\"", "product\
id": "", "vendorid": "V00", "serialnum": ""}, {"name": "\"Slot 35\"", "\
desc": "\"NX-OSv Chassis Fan Module\"", "productid": "", "vendorid": "V\
00", "serialnum": ""}]}}}
```

This example is a simple data pipeline. What are the benefits of using Kafka for data pipelines? Here are some of the benefits:

- We can produce and consume data at different time intervals. For example, some systems might want to consume data in one large bulk once a day, while others might want sub-second deliveries.
- This is perhaps the most significant benefit, for a well-maintained Kafka cluster, we can avoid a single point of failure on our data pipeline.
- We can withstand different data throughput. Just like different time intervals, some data transformations might be big, and some might be small. Kafka treated all messages as ByteArrays and simplified our storage concerns to just storing 'bytes on a disk.'
- Often, data pipeline needs to deal with different data formats. Kafka can tolerate different data formats because it is agnostic about XML, JSON, relational database format, or anything else.

As we can see, this data pipe can get pretty complicated. As we start to chain more steps toward data transformation, enhancement, adding and mutate different fields, there will always seem to be 'one more thing to add.' It is a balancing act of when and where to add a new transformation. But a major benefit of this approach is, again, the separation of concerns. We can now have one script that deals with finance department enhancement, one with security enhancement, one with operation data, and so on.

One way to simplify the data chaining complexity is to use Kafka Connect, which allows us to re-use repeatable code created by the community. So we will take a look at the next example with Kafka Connect.

Network Log as a Service

In the next example, we will treat the network log as a service. This is the overall flow:

1. Store network log as a log file.
2. We will use Kafka to read from the log file whenever new contents are added.
3. We will push the data in the topic to the Elasticsearch container we created at the beginning of the chapter.

For this example, we will use Kafka Connect.

Kafka Connect

What is Kafka Connect? As Kafka becomes popular in its adaptation, many data sources and destinations are shared amongst the community users. For example, many users want to read from SQL databases or AWS S3 buckets, enrich and transform data, then output the data to Elasticsearch or another AWS S3 bucket. It became obvious that there is value in providing a common, sharable component that everybody can use, so the users do not need to reinvent the wheels.

Kafka Connect provides an interface for commonly used datastores. It is a free, open-source component that provides data integration between popular databases, search indexes, and file systems.

There are many supported connectors, both from companies such as Confluent as well as community-provided connectors. For a partial list of supported connectors, consult the provider's documentation such as Confluent's list of supported connectors[66]. In our first Kafka Connect example, we will use the file connect both as source and destination.

Kafka File Connector Example

Kafka Connect ships with Kafka, so there is nothing new to install. To run Kafka Connect, we simply need to provide the configuration parameters and run it as another process on the same server.

> For production service, run Kafka Connect on a separate server, as you would normally do for distributed systems.

Let's move the Kafka Connect configuration file from our previous download to our current directory. I am going to rename it to *ch6_connect-distributed.properties*:

```
$ cp ~/kafka_2.13-2.8.0/config/connect-distributed.properties ch6_conne\
ct-distributed.properties
```

We do not need to change any parameters at this time, but let's take a look at what are the available parameters in this file:

- bootstrap.servers: This specifies the Kafka broker.
- group.id: All workers with the same Group ID are part of the same Connect cluster.
- key.converter and value.converter: By default, Connect uses JSON data format.

[66]https://docs.confluent.io/cloud/current/connectors/index.html

We can run the connect worker by the *connect-distributed.sh* script. We also need to specify the configuration file:

```
$ connect-distributed.sh ch6_connect-distributed.properties
...
[2021-11-07 07:45:19,380] INFO REST resources initialized; server is st\
arted and ready to handle requests (org.apache.kafka.connect.runtime.re\
st.RestServer:319)
[2021-11-07 07:45:19,380] INFO Kafka Connect started (org.apache.kafka.\
connect.runtime.Connect:57)
```

Kafka Connect provides a REST API that we can connect to the worker:

```
$ curl http://localhost:8083
{"version":"2.8.0","commit":"ebb1d6e21cc92130","kafka_cluster_id":"JSY5\
jLsCSYOH6_0PJ5d_DA"}
```

Kafka Connect uses different plugins as connectors for different data sources and destinations. The destinations are called sinks. We can view the current connector plugins, by default, we have the file source (org.apache.kafka.connect.file.FileStreamSourceConnector) and file sink (org.apache.kafka.connect.file.FileStreamSinkConnector) which allows us to read files, put its contents to a topic, and output the messages as another file:

```
$ curl http://localhost:8083/connector-plugins
[{"class":"org.apache.kafka.connect.file.FileStreamSinkConnector","type\
":"sink","version":"2.8.0"},{"class":"org.apache.kafka.connect.file.Fil\
eStreamSourceConnector","type":"source","version":"2.8.0"},{"class":"or\
g.apache.kafka.connect.mirror.MirrorCheckpointConnector","type":"source\
","version":"1"},{"class":"org.apache.kafka.connect.mirror.MirrorHeartb\
eatConnector","type":"source","version":"1"},{"class":"org.apache.kafka\
.connect.mirror.MirrorSourceConnector","type":"source","version":"1"}]
```

We will create a new topic *ch6_topic_file_connector* for our first example:

```
$ kafka-topics.sh --zookeeper 127.0.0.1:2181 --topic ch6_topic_file_con\
nector --create --partitions 3 --replication-factor 1
```

For our source file, we will create a new file, *ch6_test_file.txt*, with some test content inside:

```
$ cat ch6_test_file.txt
Hello, I am a test file for Kafka Connect file connectors.
```

We will use Kafka Connect's REST URI, *http://localhost:8083/connectors*, to specify the test file to be read with the configurations:

```
$ echo '{"name": "load-ch6-test-file", "config": {"connector.class": "F\
ileStreamSourceConnector", "file": "ch6_test_file.txt", "topic": "ch6_t\
opic_file_connector"}}' | curl -X POST -d @- http://localhost:8083/conn\
ectors --header "Content-Type:application/json"
```

We can use the file output plugin for the output file. Notice in the output file plugin, the configuration for the topic is a plural form of 'topics' instead of 'topic':

```
$ echo '{"name": "dump-ch6-test-file", "config": {"connector.class": "F\
ileStreamSinkConnector", "file": "output-of-ch6-test-file", "topics": "\
ch6_topic_file_connector"}}' | curl -X POST -d @- http://localhost:8083\
/connectors --header "Content-Type:application/json"
```

After all the work, we now have a shiny new replica of the file named dump-ch6-test-file. The beauty is the connector continuously watches for new contents made to the original file. So if we tail the new file and watch for new additions:

```
$ tail -f dump-ch6-test-file
```

When we write contents to the original file, such as updating it with logs, the new content will automatically be pushed to Kafka topic and being updated on the new file. This is really amazing! With only a few lines of configuration, we have a working publisher-subscriber queue working.

If you'd like, we can delete connector configurations via the DELETE method *http://localhost:8083/connectors/<connector name>*:

```
$ curl -X DELETE http://localhost:8083/connectors/load-ch6-test-file
$ curl -X DELETE http://localhost:8083/connectors/dump-ch6-test-file
```

Kafka Connector has lots of other connector plugins, as we saw from the Confluent list. Let's see how we can install the Elasticsearch Sink connector in the following example.

Kafka Elasticsearch Connector Example

The installation steps for the Kafka Elasticsearch Sink connector is listed on the Confluent ELasticsearch Sink connector page[67]. The easiest way is to use the Confluent Hub client.

[67] https://www.confluent.io/hub/confluentinc/kafka-connect-elasticsearch?_ga=2.175956962.1328561122.1636139861-2001896864.1629854130

We can download the Confluent Hub client in the tar zip file, then unzip and untar it to our current directory:

```
$ curl -O http://client.hub.confluent.io/confluent-hub-client-latest.ta\
r.gz
$ tar -xvzf confluent-hub-client-latest.tar.gz
```

We should have a /bin directory within the confluent-hub client directory:

```
$ ls bin/
confluent-hub
```

Let's install the Elasticsearch connector plugin.

Install Elasticsearch connector

The Confluent Hub client will download the plugin to a directory. Next, we will create a new directory under */opt* to store the connector and make the directory writable:

```
$ sudo mkdir /opt/connectors
$ sudo chmod +w /opt/connectors/
```

We can now start the download with the *–component-dir* point to the */opt/connectors* directory and *–worker-configs* point to our Kafka Connect configuration file:

```
$ sudo ./bin/confluent-hub install confluentinc/kafka-connect-elasticse\
arch:11.1.4 --component-dir /opt/connectors --worker-configs /home/echo\
u/kafka-python/ch6_connect-distributed.properties
...
Downloading component Kafka Connect Elasticsearch 11.1.4, provided by C\
onfluent, Inc. from Confluent Hub and installing into /opt/connectors
Adding installation directory to plugin path in the following files:
  /home/echou/kafka-python/ch6_connect-distributed.properties
...
Completed
```

After installation, we can run the Kafka Connect worker again. Now, when we query the plugins, we will see the Elasticsearch plugin (io.confluent.connect.elasticsearch.ElasticsearchSinkConnector) included in the output:

```
$ curl http://localhost:8083/connector-plugins
[{"class":"io.confluent.connect.elasticsearch.ElasticsearchSinkConnecto\
r","type":"sink","version":"11.1.4"},{"class":"org.apache.kafka.connect\
.file.FileStreamSinkConnector","type":"sink","version":"2.8.0"},{"class\
":"org.apache.kafka.connect.file.FileStreamSourceConnector","type":"sou\
rce","version":"2.8.0"},
...
]
```

Let's create a new topic, *ch6_topic_network_log*, for our next example:

```
$ kafka-topics.sh --zookeeper 127.0.0.1:2181 --topic ch6_topic_network_\
log --create --partitions 3 --replication-factor 1
```

We will create a network log file, *ch6_network_log.log*, as the file source:

```
$ head ch6_network_log.log
2021 Nov  6 16:16:05 lax-cor-r1 %SYSLOG-2-SYSTEM_MSG : Syslogs wont be \
logged in
to logflash until logflash is online
2021 Nov  6 16:16:07 lax-cor-r1  %USER-3-SYSTEM_MSG: ^Iaddress: <127.1.\
1.1> 7f01
0101  - in.tftpd
2021 Nov  6 16:16:08 lax-cor-r1 %KERN-3-SYSTEM_MSG: [    0.000000] Unkn\
own boot
option `ide_generic.probe_mask=0x0': ignoring - kernel
2021 Nov  6 16:16:08 lax-cor-r1 %KERN-3-SYSTEM_MSG: [    0.395120] pci \
0000:00:0
1.0: PIIX3: Enabling Passive Release - kernel
2021 Nov  6 16:16:08 lax-cor-r1 %KERN-3-SYSTEM_MSG: [   18.095426] klm_\
cmos:672
- ERR: sysconf2 checksum failed expected 0x0, got 0xff - kernel
```

As we have done before, we can configure the file connector for this log file as the source:

```
$ echo '{"name": "load-network-log", "config": {"connector.class": "Fil\
eStreamSourceConnector", "file": "ch6_network_log.log", "topic": "ch6_t\
opic_network_log"}}' | curl -X POST -d @- http://localhost:8083/connect\
ors --header "Content-Type:application/json"
```

Unlike the first example, we can now specify Elasticsearch as the sink destination. We need to make sure both Elasticsearch and Kibana containers are running; refer to the earlier sections if needed:

```
$ echo '{"name": "network-log-elastic-sink", "config": {"connector.clas\
s": "ElasticsearchSinkConnector", "connection.url": "http://localhost:9\
200", "type.name": "_doc", "topics": "ch6_topic_network_log", "key.igno\
re": true}}' | curl -X POST -d @- http://localhost:8083/connectors --he\
ader "Content-Type:application/json"
```

If we now go back to our Kibana dashboard and hoover under *Kibana -> Index Patterns -> Create New Index Pattern*, we will see the new *ch6_-topic_network_log* index in Elasticsearch:

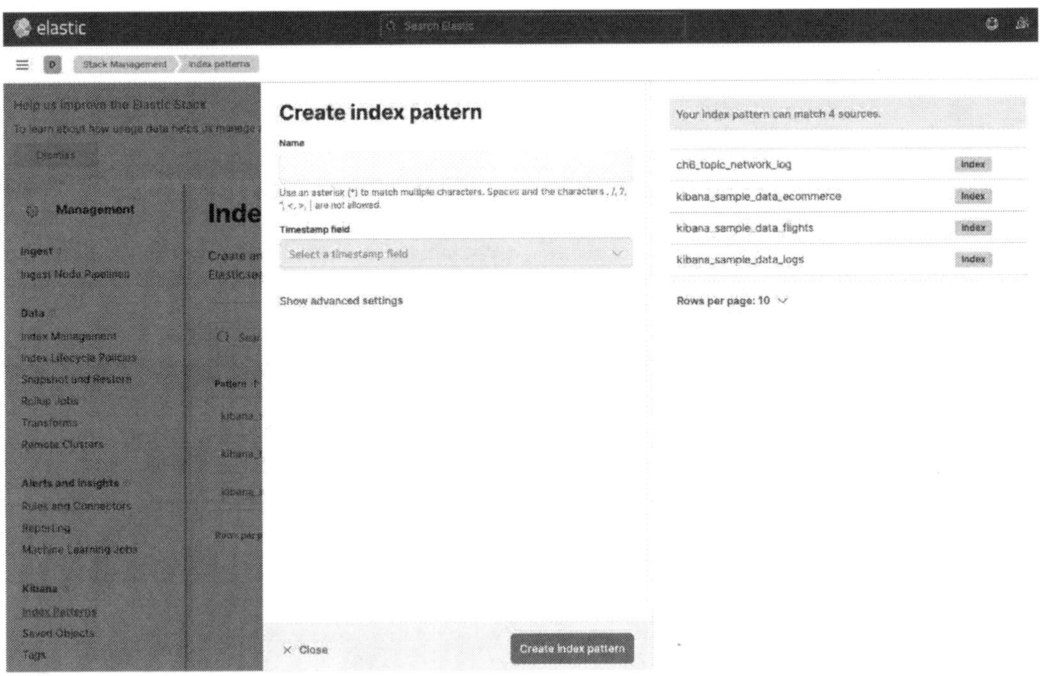

Figure 6.5 Elastic Create Index Patterns

This workflow is admittedly the most complex in the book so far. I have had multiple attempts to get everything working correctly. This example requires all the components: Kafka cluster, Kafka Connect, Connect Plugins, Docker Engine, Elasticsearch container, and Kibana container to be working.

Elasticsearch and Kibana might also look strange if you have not used them before. But this is how real-world data pipelines usually are. They are messy and sometimes fragile, the stars have to align for it to work.

In building this example, I used all the tools we have learned so far for troubleshooting. If you run into issues, here are some troubleshooting ideas. First, we can use the Kafka Connector URI endpoint to make sure the connectors are loaded:

```
$ curl 'localhost:8083/connectors'
["network-log-elastic-sink","load-network-log"]
```

We can also check the specific connector configuration:

```
$ curl 'localhost:8083/connectors/network-log-elastic-sink/config'
{"connector.class":"ElasticsearchSinkConnector","type.name":"true","top\
ics":"ch6_topic_network_log","tasks.max":"1","name":"network-log-elasti\
c-sink","connection.url":"http://localhost:9200","key.ignore":"true","s\
chema.ignore":"true"}
```

Don't forget we can use the reliable console producer to manually produce some log messages to the topic when the file connector does not seem to work:

```
$ kafka-console-producer.sh --broker-list 127.0.0.1:9092 --topic ch6_to\
pic_network_log
...
>{"name":"Test log 2", "severity": "WARN"}
...
```

We can also use the console consumer to watch for new messages appear on the topic:

```
$ kafka-console-consumer.sh --bootstrap-server 127.0.0.1:9092 --topic c\
h6_topic_network_log --group consumer_group_1 --property parse.key=true
...
{"name":"Test log 2", "severity": "WARN"}
...
```

Finally, once we are happy with the result, we can delete the connectors:

```
$ curl -X DELETE http://localhost:8083/connectors/load-network-log
$ curl -X DELETE http://localhost:8083/connectors/network-log-elastic-s\
ink
```

This example was a challenging one, congratulations on making it work! Do not be discouraged if there are some additional tweaks to be done. As far as putting it into production, the workflow is completed, but there is more work to be done on the message format. On the Elasticsearch end, we will need to add a timestamp field and possibly other fields. But that is outside of the scope of this book, please feel free to check out the Elasticsearch Guide[68] for additional information.

Conclusion

In this chapter, we put everything we have learned so far in the book. We tried out different ways we could apply Kafka in our network engineering journey. We began the chapter by integrating network device queries with Kafka producer and consumer. We then built a simple data pipeline by using multiple topics and external information to enhance the data.

Later in the chapter, we use Kafka Connect to use the reusable ways to ingest and output data to different sources. The file source and file

[68]https://www.elastic.co/guide/en/elasticsearch/reference/current/index.html

sink connectors were shipped with Kafka, and we used them to test out continuously reading from file and continuously output to file. In the last section, we installed the Elasticsearch connector plugin and used it in our data pipeline.

In the next chapter, we will take a look at some additional topics regarding Kafka and where to go for more information.

Chapter 7. Other Kafka Considerations and Looking Ahead

In the past few years, the amount of data we collected, stored, and analyzed has increased substantially. Our applications are increasingly reliant on real-time data to provide the service our customers and partners come to appreciate. As a result, the open-source projects related to data analysis have increased in popularity and adaptation.

Kafka is one of the fastest-growing open-source message streaming platforms for data. Throughout this book, we studied Kafka's concepts, learned about its usage thru examples, using hosted Kafka services, and public cloud providers' adaptation of Kafka. We also looked at different Kafka use cases in the network engineering context.

However, we have only scratched the surface of what Kafka can do. There are also many different considerations related to hardware and configuration that we did not get to cover. In this chapter, I would like to point out some of these considerations and resources if you'd like to study Kafka further.

Hardware Considerations

Most of the hardware consideration has to do with performance. As with any performance guidance, the answer is usually "it depends." Nobody can give a one-size-fits-all solution because performance has a lot to do with the data and application in your environment. Selecting the right hardware configuration can be more art than science. However, we can think about several hardware considerations based on the Kafka architecture.

Disk

Kafka messages use the local disk to store logs, commit offsets, and messages. **The disk performance can greatly influence the performance of Kafka.** For example, most producers will wait for confirmation of message commitment from Kafka broker before moving to the following message, and Kafka broker cannot send confirmation until it is committed to local storage. The faster the broker can write to its disk, the faster it can send the confirmation.

The obvious decision when it comes to disk is to use **solid-state disks (SSD)** for faster performance. Of course, SSDs are generally more expensive than traditional hard drives (HDD), so we are making a trade-off between capacity and performance.

Another area to think about is the disk format. When possible, choose to format the disk with XFS[69]. It has a higher performance in terms of reads and writes.

Memory

Kafka uses Java Heap for operations as well as system memory for OS page cache. The recommendation is to set *KAFKA_HEAP_OPTS* environmental to 4GB or more:

[69]https://en.wikipedia.org/wiki/XFS

```
export KAFKA_HEAP_OPTS="-Xmx4g"
```

We should also disable *vm.swappiness* for Kafka servers:

```
vm.swappiness=1
```

Network and CPU

As network engineers, we know distributed systems rely on networks heavily to perform well. For Kafka, network latency is essential, which means we need to give it as much bandwidth as possible and ideally not share it with other bandwidth-heavy applications.

For CPU, processing power is generally not as crucial to Kafka as other hardware such as Disk and RAM. CPU only comes into play if we are using SSL for connections, and Kafka Broker needs to encrypt and decrypt every payload. Generally speaking, CPU performance would not be a bottleneck if we exercise good housekeeping for the system, such as Garbage Collection over time.

Kafka Broker and Topic Configurations

Kafka Broker has many configuration options we can tweak to fit our situation. When we run in the lab, as we have done in this book, we can rely on the default options. However, there might be a time when we need to fine-tune some of the setups, a good resource for consulting is the Kafka Broker Configurations Doc on Confluent[70].

Here is a partial list of some of the configuration options, some of which we have used before:

[70] https://docs.confluent.io/platform/current/installation/configuration/broker-configs.html

broker.id: We have seen this setting before. The most important thing is for this id to be unique in our cluster.
port: If we ever want to change the listening port from 9092, we can change the port number.
zookeeper.connect: If the Broker is not registered to the intended Zookeeper, make sure this is specified correctly.
log.dirs: Kafka persists all messages to disk; specifying a directory will ensure we know where to look for data if need be.
auto.create.topics.enable: If we do not want topics to be automatically created, this is where we can turn it off.
num.partitions: I like to specify the number of partitions when creating a topic manually. However, for automatically created topics, it will follow this setting for the number of partitions to be created.
log.retention.ms: This is the most common configuration to use for how long to keep the messages. By default, it is one week.
message.max.bytes: By default, Kafka limits the message size to 1MB. We can increase this number, but keep in mind by increasing the message bytes allowed, they will increase the network latency and disk I/O throughput.

Schema Registry

As we have seen in previous examples, before the Kafka producer sends the message to the Kafka broker, it serializes the data. The Kafka message is sent and stored as ByteArrays. When the consumer receives the data, it will deserialize the data before it can be read by the application. We need serialization because it allows us to preserve the object during transmission and storage. This Confluent Article[71] goes more into the process.

[71] https://developer.confluent.io/learn-kafka/kafka-streams/serialization/

Since the data is just ByteArrays, Kafka does not check the validity of the data format or type. For example, if one of the message values is supposed to be a string and the producer sends an integer, Kafka will happily store it and send it to the consumer. The issue will only be known at the consumer end. This is obviously not ideal. Another issue is data changes over time. I remember at one point I used to own fax machines and on-call pager, which is something that might be stored as personal profiles in Kafka. Later on, when we need to change those records, it becomes a pain to deal with obsolete fields.

Schema Registry intends to solve those problems. It allows us to specify the structure, type, and meaning of the data. It is also integrated into the Kafka producer serializer to catch any potential error, i.e., sending integer in a string field, early on.

Schema Registry lives outside of Kafka. To use schema registry, the producers and consumers will talk to schema registries, such as Confluent's Schema Registry, to send and receive schemas that describe the data model:

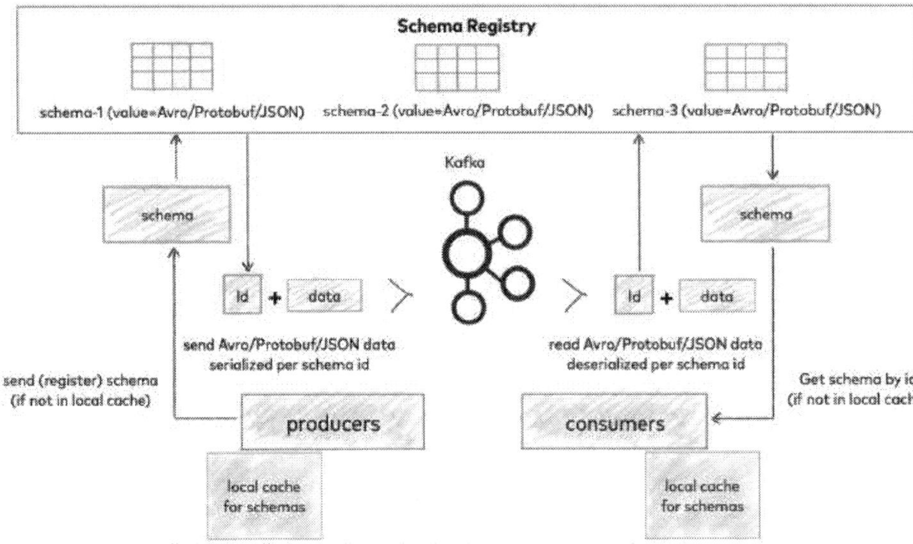

Confluent Schema Registry for storing and retrieving schemas

Confluent Schema Registry (source: https://docs.confluent.io/platform/current/schema-registry/index.html)

For more information on Schema Registry, please reference the Confluent Schema Registry article[72].

Kafka Stream Processing

According to Confluent's documentation[73]: "Kafka Streams is a client library for building applications and microservices, where the input and output data are stored in an Apache Kafka cluster. It combines the simplicity of writing and deploying standard Java and Scala applications on the client-side with the benefit of Kafka's server-side cluster technology".

In other words, when we start to have multiple steps in a continuous

[72]https://docs.confluent.io/platform/current/schema-registry/index.html
[73]https://docs.confluent.io/platform/current/streams/index.html

flow of data, we want to leverage a common library to take care of the steps. For example, when we receive log data from our network devices, we might want to correlate the source with our inventory database, transform the management IP to a readable hostname, external lookup IP via GeoIP database, and check against a blacklist of IPs. If we have several of these streams, it might start to get complicated.

Kafka Stream can help us manage the data stream pipeline in terms of topology, design, and event processing. The document Kafka Streams Overview[74] is a good starting point to learn more about it.

Cross-Cluster Data Mirroring

Throughout this book, we have been dealing with a single cluster. It is complicated enough to learn how Kafka works in a single cluster. There is really not enough space to cover cross-cluster data mirroring. However, cross-cluster data replication might be a topic that came up during the initial evaluation of using Kafka in the environment.

The good news is there is an open-source project called MirrorMaker[75] that aims at maintaining a replica of the existing Kafka cluster. The project also includes different considerations (regional vs. central, cloud, latency) and possible topology (hub-and-spoke, active-active).

Additional Resources

There are a number of good resources if you'd like to learn more about Kafka:

[74] https://docs.confluent.io/platform/current/streams/index.html

[75] https://cwiki.apache.org/confluence/pages/viewpage.action?pageId=27846330

- Kafka documentation: The Officia Apache Kafka Documentation[76] is a great place to consult for design, implementation, operations, and all things related to Kafka.
- Kafka The Definitive Guide book: At the time of the writing, Confluent provides a free download of the book Kafka: The Definitive Guide[77] by O'Reilly Publishing. This is an excellent source of knowledge written by one of the co-inventors of Kafka.
- Kafka Udemy Courses: I would highly recommend Stephane Maarek's Udemy Courses[78] if you are interested in taking more courses on Kafka.

Of course, this is just a partial list of resources to learn more about Kafka. A simple search online would yield hundreds of available resources, if not more. But the resources listed here are the ones I have personally gone thru and can validate their quality.

Conclusion

We have reached the end of the book. This has been a new experiment for me. This book was a result of me learning, implementing, and taking down notes while trying to work on a project related to Kafka. Breaking away from my previous book publishing experience, I wanted to use a platform that allows me the flexibility to update content as frequently as I feel the need. I had a lot of fun writing this book, and I hope you enjoy reading it as much as I did writing it.

Thank you for your time. For any feedback, please feel free to write to *book-feedback@networkautomationnerds.com*. I wish you the best of

[76] https://kafka.apache.org/documentation/

[77] https://www.confluent.io/resources/kafka-the-definitive-guide/

[78] https://www.udemy.com/user/stephane-maarek/

luck in your networking journey.

Appendix A. Installing Lab Instance in Public Cloud

If you would like to use public cloud virtual machines to run the Kafka lab instance, there are just a few more things to think about. The steps for installing Zookeeper and Kafka Brokers on the single server do not change. If you run the console consumer and console producer on the same machine, there is no change either.

However, the biggest issue that trips people up, myself included, is when we need to access the server remotely. We need to modify the *advertised.listeners* accordingly to the external IP or the DNS name for the EC2 host. This is due to the fact that if left unchanged, the EC2 host will advertise the private IP toward the remote client, which will not be reachable.

The Public IPv4 DNS name of the EC2 host can be seen on the instance detail page:

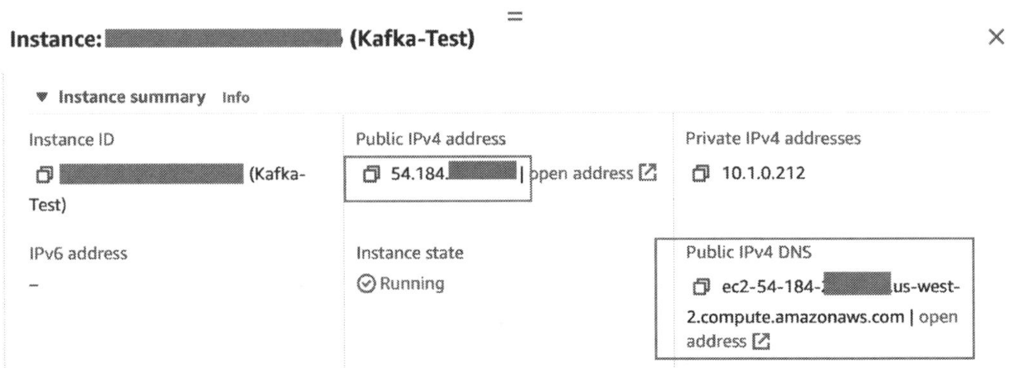

Figure Appendix A. 1 EC2 Public IPv4 DNS

We will need to change the *server.properties* accordingly under *advertised.listeners*:

```
# Hostname and port the broker will advertise to producers and consumer\
s. If not set,
# it uses the value for "listeners" if configured.  Otherwise, it will \
use the value
# returned from java.net.InetAddress.getCanonicalHostName().
advertised.listeners=PLAINTEXT://ec2-54-184-<name>.us-west-2.compute.am\
azonaws.com:9092
```

Another thing to look out for is security groups. My recommendation would be to limit the SSH and port 9092 access to known /32 IPs.

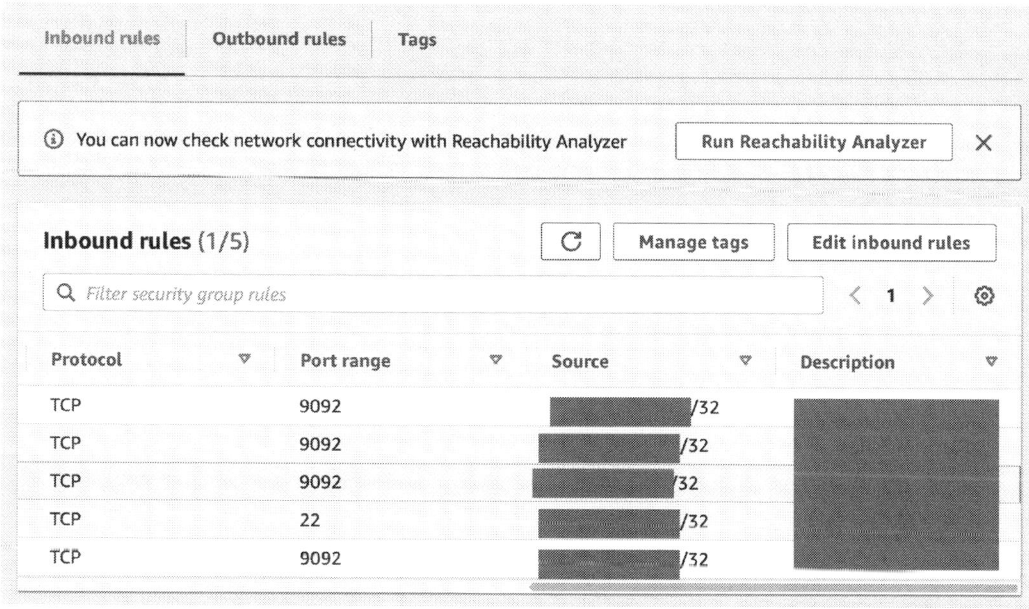

Figure Appendix A. 2 Security Inbound Rules

Kafka security is not the easiest thing to configure, especially for beginners. Limiting access via the AWS security group is, in my opinion, a better way to go without spending too much time on encryption, keys, certificates, and other security-related settings. However, if you are unable to limit just by IP, or if you would like to read up more on Kafka security, please feel free to take a look at the Confluent documentation[79].

[79]https://docs.confluent.io/3.0.0/kafka/security.html

Made in the USA
Monee, IL
13 September 2026

62976625R00096